5,00

CONSCIOUSNESS
AND
TRADITION

Jacob Needleman

CONSCIOUSNESS AND TRADITION

CROSSROAD · NEW YORK

1982
The Crossroad Publishing Company
575 Lexington Avenue, New York, NY 10022

Library of Congress Cataloging in Publication Data

Needleman, Jacob.
Conciousness and tradition.

Includes index.
1. Philosophy—Addresses, essays, lectures.
2. Religion—Addresses, essays, lectures.
I. Title.
B29.N36   190   81–17243
ISBN 0–8245–0453–4   AACR2

For Benn and Ruth

CONTENTS

INTRODUCTION

THE year is 1955, the place Harvard University. I have just begun my senior year, majoring in philosophy, and am on my way to the first meeting of the fall semester classes. One course especially intrigues me—a graduate seminar in Hinduism. The instructor, I have learned, is one of India's most eminent philosophers and is visiting Harvard for one semester only.

Will I be admitted to the course? Undergraduates are permitted to sign up for such seminars at Harvard, but only with the instructor's approval. Will there be room for me? Will my academic preparation be considered adequate?

I enter Emerson Hall, a stolid, ivy-covered building, passing under portals inscribed with the words, "What is man that thou art mindful of him?"* In these classrooms I have broken my head over Hegel's *Phenomenology of Mind.* I have seen my adolescent love of Spinoza smothered by historical analysis. I have been driven toward intellectual schizophrenia by the greatness of Plato and the exposure of his "inconsistencies" through the latest techniques of language analysis. I have sweated and even wept trying to gain command of *The Critique of Pure Reason,* finally breaking through with the help of two week's supply of Dexadrine. I have been transported studying Kierkegaard, only to be told that he was not really a philosopher. I have played with symbolic logic as though it were a toy, only to be told it is the key to reasoning about the fundamental questions of human life.

Here, in short, in these classrooms, I have become modern, contemporary. God? A powerful, but outdated, myth. Ethics? A systematic justification of arbitrary preferences. Metaphysics? A disease of language. Every educated person should of course know about these things in

---

* Legend has it, however, that the real world view of Emerson Hall is hidden somewhere under the ivy: "Man is the measure of all things."

order to understand the past and in order to appreciate the richness of Western culture. Knowing about these things and learning how to investigate and criticize is good, is necessary. Think, study, explore, analyze. Perhaps it is going to lead somewhere, perhaps not, but in itself it is good: it is connected to what is highest in man.

And now here I am sitting in an empty classroom waiting for a Hindu professor to bring into this same building the culture of the Orient. Along with nervousness about being admitted to the course, I feel that same shadowy kind of hope I experienced at the start of my courses in Plato, Spinoza, and Kierkegaard. Down deep, I want something bigger than my own mind. But at the same time I am eager to put all great ideas into my pocket—or, as it is said, to "master" them. It is the way I have been trained. How else to approach great ideas? And yet, there is that strange hope for something bigger and greater than myself. Will the mysticism of India also be contained by the classrooms of Emerson Hall?

I begin to wonder if I have arrived at the wrong time. I check my watch and the class schedule. All in order. Then where is everyone? I get up and pace around the room and finally peer out the doorway into the high, dark corridors. A tiny, slender man is just then coming through the entrance arch. It must be him. Quickly, I dart back into the classroom and take a seat at the rear of the room, avoiding the large, circular seminar table.

The little man walks into the classroom with measured steps and takes his seat at the front of the seminar table. He puts a folder of papers in front of him along with several small, dark blue books and then looks up at me. He tilts his head and begins to speak: "Out text this semester will be *The Subject as Freedom* by K. C. Bhattacharya. It is a very difficult book and we will proceed line by line. Please take a copy."

I awkwardly rise from my chair, bumping against the folded-out armrest, nearly overturning the chair in the process. Horrible sounds echo in the room. Taking the book from his outstretched hand, I am met by a pair of luminous eyes set far back in a bony, brown face that shows little signs of age apart from the whiteness of hair. The teeth are white and gleaming. He motions me to sit next to him and instructs me to open the book to Chapter One: "The Notion of Subjectivity."

I cannot believe what is happening. I am the only student taking the course! Out there, other classrooms are filled with undergraduates signed up for courses in British Empiricism, Deductive Logic, Political Philosophy, Aristotle, Existentialism, and all the other items on the menu of La Maison de Philosophie Occidentale. Graduate students are packing seminar rooms to study Wittgenstein, Frege, Russell, and Carnap. For a moment, I feel like a fool. Are they right after all? Why should anyone want to study Hinduism? Do the teachings of the East even deserve to be called philosophy? Don't they, and Hinduism especially, represent all that is obscure and confused in man's efforts to deal with the mysteries of life and the world?

I stayed. I carried that book around with me day and night, and I still have it. The pages are black with underlinings and marginal notes blurred by time. The binding is torn and held together with brittle Scotch tape and an old rubber band. Just the other day I looked at it again as I sat down to work on the introduction to these essays. And I began reading it with astonishment. It is nothing less than an attempt to express the metaphysics and epistemology of yoga in modern philosophical, scientific language. The author is trying to prove, logically, that the problems of mind, nature, and ethics that have bedeviled Western thought since the Renaissance can only be solved through the ancient spiritual discipline of awareness. No wonder I never understood a word of it.

Is it true? Is the science of awareness what has been missing from all our thought and life since the dawn of the modern era?

This question, in any case, forms the backbone of the present volume. Now, seeing these essays of mine collected together for the first time, I am astonished by the commonality of this question throughout. Whether the subject is the condition of modern philosophy, or the resurgent interest in religious traditions, or the contrast between ancient and modern systems of medicine, or the problems of how to live in a technocentric world, in every case the culminating or reconciling idea is that modern man has forgotten how to cultivate the power of awareness of himself; he has even forgotten what awareness is.

I did not intend it that way. When writing these essays, I was addressing questions and issues that often seemed at first glance to have nothing much to do with awareness. That this is what each issue led to either says something about the author's fixation or about awareness itself, namely, that it is inherently a hidden answer to the questions of life, an answer or a direction that emerges only when the mind comes to the end of its tether and all its usual patterns of thought have proved fruitless.

Much in our world, much in our modern way of living, is "at the end of its tether." Not only philosophy, but medicine, religion, and technology have reached a profound impasse where motion accelerates, but without direction. Almost every human endeavor, every pattern and form of life—art, business, government, the family, work, ethics, education—seems to have broken from its moorings. And every one of us is riding in one of these rapidly accelerating vessels, looking for a way, a direction, and a means of guiding it and ourselves.

At the same time, for most modern people, the term "awareness" conveys no clear meaning or sense of hope. There are good reasons for this. What we conceive under this term has proved itself, on the whole, to be as powerless to transform our personal or collective situation as anything else that has been offered over the years by religion, science, psychology, or political ideology. Awareness, or consciousness, has been variously identified with one or another form of mind activity and set over against such faculties as will, passion, and feeling. It has been identified with intellection, reasoning, the gathering of information. It has been equated with scientific, philosophic, or artistic insight and expression. When so defined, it simply appears as another name for many of the things our culture has already tried both in and outside of Emerson Hall. Undefined, the term leads us nowhere; defined, it reads out like an old story we are tired of hearing. In addition, the use of this term among current new-age thinkers has already taken on a dreamy quality mingling bits and pieces of mysticism, romanticism, and old-fashioned programmatic enthusiasm.

The essays in this volume are offered as evidence that awareness cannot be understood simply as an alternative to anything our culture has tried and is still trying. The question is, rather: Is it possible to see ourselves without prematurely explaining ourselves? Does not this effort itself loom as an entirely different direction of the mind and heart of man—just to see, without program or position, what we are as individuals and as a civilization?

There are traditional words associated with this latent power of the mind. But these terms almost invariably appear in association with an attitude that is exceedingly difficult for modern people to accept—an attitude that appears as aloofness or noninvolvement. In Buddhism there is the term *emptiness*; there is Meister Eckhardt's *Abgeschiedenheit* (indifference) and the *apatheia* of the early fathers of the contemplative Christian tradition; there is the *sobriety* of the Sufis and, of course, the *detachment* of Hinduism. Yet the real context of these terms is always the most deeply felt concern for the human problem. They always occur within the ambit of a way offered to man to escape from and transcend his suffering, ignorance, and immorality. Paradoxically, the most glorious compassion and care for man is associated with the most complete separation from the vortex of man's life in the world. Connected to this, but even more of a seeming paradox, the greatest vision of a reality beyond the appearance of this world is associated with a pure and exact awareness of those very appearances.

Consider this characterization of the Buddhist tradition in Tibet:

> Meditation, considered as the foundational act of spiritual effort in the Vajrayana tradition as transmitted by Milarepa, may also be considered in terms of the possible development within man of a link between the Buddha nature and the ordinary deluded mind. The great idea behind this notion of a relationship between the highest and lowest in human nature, which (we are told) only the greatest masters have realized, is expressed in the Vajrayana as the essential identity of nirvana [the state of transcendent liberation] and samsara [the prison of delusion and suffering]: *nirvana is the understanding of samsara!**

When we speak of awareness as something modern man has not yet tried, we are speaking of a strange and powerful intermingling: a deep immersion in human experience together with a radical separation from it. The essays in this book have turned out to be, almost without my intending it, efforts to reach toward this paradox. We are speaking here of a paradox in the heart of reality itself, or shall we say, a contradiction in the heart of reality itself.

How can that be? In any case, I wish to reserve the term "sacred" for that helping force which reconciles this contradiction in ourselves and in the universe itself.

But how can we speak of a paradox at the heart of reality? We can accept, perhaps, that the greatest saints and sages of the world have exhibited this breathtaking contradiction in their own being—an extraordinary, passionate involvement in the whole life of man together with a luminous detachment from it, a profound outward movement coexisting with an equally profound inward movement. What contains these two contradictory movements within one human being? Whatever it is, surely the meaning of the sacred lies there.

Do these two movements exist also at the heart of reality as contradictory energies? If so, then what word shall we use to designate their reconciliation? Shall we speak of this reconciling energy as *spirit* or the Christ principle or as Christ himself?

But saying this, I seem to feel the walls of Emerson Hall closing in, the premature explanation, the conceptual fitting together of that which needs to be suffered and experienced in all its contradiction before any

---

* *Introduction* to *The Life of Milarepa*, trans. Lobsang P. Lhalungpa (London: Granada Publishing, 1979), p. xix.

hope of real reconciliation or harmonization can appear. Surely, it is possible to say that our modern world, a world at the end of its tether, is in a position to recognize the ultimacy of this contradiction. Surely, we have had enough of premature pseudoreconciliations in the form of abstractions, theories, or philosophies that attempt to close the whole of living reality in a narrow system. But we have suffered equally from attempts to flee from the orderly mind into irrationalism and emotionalism.

To be silent, to wait and watch: this is the message sounded by the great masters of the traditions, Eastern and Western. We have associated this call mainly with the East, but it is very much at the core of our own Judaic and Christian teachings. But to act, to will, to become: this, too, is the call sounded by the traditions and not only those of the West. As metaphors, the East means the movement inward toward oneself; and the West means the movement outward toward the world and my neighbor. Awareness, then, is the confrontation in ourselves, and in the world, of East and West.

Can we look at life in this way, under the aegis of this contradiction? Take any aspect of our world you wish: family, religion, science, art—we see that something has come to its end, its limit. The family is threatened, religion is fragmented and unsure of itself, science brings equal parts of destruction and knowledge, art is dissolving into self-indulgent subjectivity. Everywhere people are asking, *Why?* What is the family for? What is real religion? How can science bring good to mankind? Can the artist give us vision instead of only excitement? Everywhere there is a movement to return to the origins of human life in all its various forms—a search for presuppositions, fundamental planks of living and thinking. There is a widespread sense that everything in our world has gone out too far, too far away from some center of origin, and we wish to move back and take stock.

Of course, the same drama is being played out in our daily lives as well. As individuals, we also feel that our activities are too complicated and too fragmented; we seek to step back into ourselves, toward our own original nature—yet at the same time we are drawn out more and more by the demands of living in the present age. We seek values, redefinition of aims in our own religious, academic, family, or vocational lives. We seek ethical anchors, which is only one expression among many of this impulse to move back (or up, according to our language, up toward "God").

New ideas and new theories, new insights, new mental or physical technologies, new ideologies, new causes to follow, new wars to wage—

for many of us, this cannot be the answer. This can only increase or per-
petuate the problem of the world at the end of its tether. The sacred
cannot appear in human life as only another program to follow, as only
a new alternative. If we are seeking the sacred, which means an authen-
tically higher level of understanding and living, surely it means discovering a new quality of attention to everything that now tears us apart. Is
there something, some force within the human mind, that has the power
not to be torn apart by the fragmentation of life and by the fundamental
contradiction at the heart of life? To this question the essays in this volume, taken together, answer yes—this force can exist in us as an awareness that is both silent and alive. In order to reach the harmony and
unity we long for, we must intentionally accept the contradictions we
are born to.

A thousand years ago, the masters of the Sufi brotherhood known as
the Ikhwan al-Safa (Brethren of Purity) or Khillan al-Wafa (Friends of
Sincerity) were articulating the same message. In their writings they tell
the story of a disillusioned worshiper who is brought to the point of at-
tributing malice to God for ordering his creation in this way. Seeing that
he is pulled apart by opposing forces all equally embedded in God's
creation, he cries out, "O God, Thou hast brought together contradictory elements, mutually pulling and repelling forces! I know no more
what to do or how, lost as I am between them!" God responds first by
pointing to the moral faculties he has given man that enable him to steer
a middle course in life. He then reminds man of the *Namus,* the revealed
law, which he has sent down to man through his prophets. But, as for the
deepest and most fundamental contradictions of existence, he instructs
man that they have been placed there not to be resolved but to be lived
in full consciousness of their contradictoriness.

In our era, it was Kierkegaard who restated this vision as definitive of
the human condition and as offering the only path toward possibilities
locked within the structure of human nature. The Self, said Kierkegaard, in an oft-quoted, but variously interpreted passage, is a synthesis
of two contradictory levels—the finite and the infinite, the temporal and
the eternal. But, says Kierkegaard, man has not yet seen and accepted,
has not yet willed, his two opposing natures. And, mysteriously, paradoxically, to do so is for man the only means of grounding himself
transparently (in full consciousness), in the Power which posited the self,
which created man. It is not enough to be good in an ethical sense. Beyond the ethical, beyond the choice of the "good" in human life, and the
concomitant exclusion of the "evil," there lies a mysterious act of existential spirituality, a struggle to accept the whole of our individual life

and structure with all its fragmentation and many-leveled contradiction. In that struggle for awareness and acceptance, God is discovered within ourselves as a Power that is both wholly other and wholly myself. Call this Power *spirit*.

Kierkegaard, in his time, stood practically alone in his effort to show that the harmonization of human life cannot take place through the instrumentality of thought alone. His attack on Hegel can be understood, of course, from precisely that point of view. For this, he has been wrongly labeled irrationalist. But the awareness and act of will he speaks of is not irrational. On the contrary, what he is speaking of is the same thing that was spoken of in an earlier era as active Mind, the agent intellect, whereas what modern man calls thought is little more than one of many natural mechanisms by which the active intellect moves through existence.

Translated into contemporary terms, the message of Kierkegaard remains something *we have not yet tried*. The solutions offered by science, psychiatry, conventional religion, political ideology are the contemporary version of the ethical, the "good." That is to say, they exclude the "evil," they are overwhelmed and refuted by "evil," by the fact of the world, by the way the world actually goes—with all its war, violence, injustice, and destruction. We have not yet found, or even sought for, the active Mind, the awareness that calls forth a Power through its complete attention to the whole of reality. This world is also myself.

The whole of Kierkegaard's life, an amazing kaleidoscope of reason and feeling, introspection, analysis, faith, rebellion, self-doubt, moral yearning, sexual suffering, and luminous understanding, is an indication and a warning about this awareness and will which man has not yet tried. In short, it is not *easy*. It is immensely difficult, and difficult even in a way we do not understand, yet also simple in a way we do not understand. It is a surrender which is not merely passive; an effort that is without the tensions of the ego. And it involves a life lived in all its humanness.

Like many of my peers, I was at first drawn only to the irrationalist interpretation of Kierkegaard. Disillusioned with Emerson Hall, I became an existentialist. I imagined that I was following Kierkegaard in his attack on Hegel and I found philosophies ready to support this picture of myself. But was there not something fundamentally right or healthy even in this lopsided picture? Existentialism seemed to offer the inclusion of real life, passion, feeling, pleasure, and pain, all of that in the world of ideas and pondering. This impulse to include more of life, more of actual experience in the activity of the mind was indeed a right direction. But, as the essay "Man's Nature and Natural Man" indicates, existentialism itself eventually proved too nonexistentialist. Without knowing why, I began to suffer again from the question of how to include the whole of life in consciousness; the question of how to *be*; the question of *being* in the midst of *becoming*.

I am still seeking the answer to this question. But I know now that the whole world is seeking it as well, or, in any case, suffering from the failure to face this question of *being* in the midst of becoming, the search for a center of selfhood that both clarifies and transcends the pulls, shocks, and contradictions of everyday existence. I am convinced that every central problem in the world, external and internal, needs to be seen in the light of this question about an awareness of the forces and movements rooted in the heart of being. To search for the sacred in life is, in this view, to search for an awareness of the real forces operating in every situation. One may hesitate to speak, as Kierkegaard spoke, of the Power that can appear when this awareness and will exist. Even he was sometimes reluctant to name it *God,* not because he doubted that God was the proper name, but because he knew how fragile this awareness and will are, how they constantly need to be rediscovered as long as one lives.

Several years ago, at the invitation of Harvey Cox, I returned to Harvard where I lectured on the subject of the new American religious movements and attended the graduate seminar he was conducting on "Spiritual Disciplines in Comparative Perspective." Speaking to nearly a hundred students about the entry into American culture of esoteric and Oriental teachings, I could not help remembering the empty classroom a few blocks away where I had my first bewildering academic experience of Eastern philosophy. I was impressed by how readily these students grasped ideas that had taken me years even to begin to understand, years of personal and intellectual wanderings, without guidance, during which I had more than once rejected the whole idea of the spiritual as the pursuit of a chimera. Would the explanations and clarifications that professors such as myself were now offering help these young people in their movement toward a search for themselves? Or had I, too, become part of Emerson Hall?

On the afternoon following my lecture, I strolled over to Harvard Yard, headed for Emerson Hall. I wandered around the classrooms, listening at the doors like any nostalgic alumnus, and then went upstairs to revisit the Philosophy Department library. I looked to see if any of the most important and recent works dealing with esoteric and Oriental ideas were on the shelves. Nothing of the kind. It was still logic, language analysis, philosophy of science, and numerous "strictly kosher" historical texts and scholarly translations.

On the way out of the building, I struck up a conversation with a student who happened to be carrying one of the books I had brought out in my Penguin Metaphysical Library series: *To Live Within* by Lizelle Reymond. This is a book of immense power and great subtlety, dealing with the realities of the spiritual search and, in the process, presenting the teachings of India in a way they have never been understood in the Western world.

"What course are you reading that book for?" I asked him.

"It's not for any course," he answered. "I'm reading it for myself."

*   *   *

The essays in this volume cover a span of about thirteen years. "Man's Nature and Natural Man" was presented at Duquesne University in 1967 and was published in *Humanitas,* Vol. IV, Number 1, Spring, 1968 (Duquesne University, Pittsburgh, Pa.). "Why Philosophy is Easy" originally appeared in *The Review of Metaphysics,* Vol. XXII, No. 1, September 1968 (Haverford College, Haverford, Pa.).

Both "The Used Religions" and "Psychiatry and the Sacred" were originally offered in two series of lectures sponsored by Far West Institute in San Francisco. The first series, held in 1972, addressed the question of whether and how the ancient spiritual traditions could speak to the contemporary world. It was published under the title *Sacred Tradition and Present Need* (ed. Jacob Needleman and Dennis Lewis, Viking Press, New York, 1972). The second series dealt with the current attempt by a growing number of psychiatrists and therapists to adapt ancient spiritual methods to psychotherapeutic ends. It was published as *On the Way to Self Knowledge* (ed. Jacob Needleman and Dennis Lewis, Alfred A. Knopf, New York, 1975). "The Art of Living in the Cultural Revolution" is published here for the first time, although it, too, was written for a public lecture series of the same name conducted under the auspices of Far West Institute. In that series of lectures, eminent men and women from the arts, sciences, business, and religion spoke of the values they sought to live by in a world constantly changing under the impact of the new technologies. This series was published as *Speaking of My Life* (ed. Jacob Needleman, Harper and Row, San Francisco, 1979). A fourth series of Far West lectures on this same theme of the art of living, featuring such speakers as Norman Cousins, John Gardner, Huston Smith, David Bohm, Laurens van der Post, and others, was broadcast on public television in 1980 and is still being repeated in various cities throughout the country. My overall debt to Far West Institute is considerable for the extraordinary manner in which it brings serious ideas to formulation and offers carefully structured conditions for exploring them.

"Magic, Sacrifice, and Tradition" and "The Two Sciences of Medicine" were first published in *Parabola* magazine (Vol. I, Number 2, Spring 1976 and Vol. III, Number 3, August 1978). The former contains ideas and experiments in literary form that later found their way into my *Lost Christianity* (Doubleday, New York, 1980). "The Two Sciences of Medicine" was originally presented at an international conference on ancient and modern medicine in Shiraz in 1977.

"The Search for a Wise Man" was written for *Search* (ed. Jean Sulzberger, Harper and Row, New York, 1980), and appeared in that volume in a somewhat shortened version. The full text is published here for the first time and my thanks are due to Miss Sulzberger for her kindness in agreeing to its publication in this volume.

"Notes on Religion" in a highly edited form comprises the entries on religion in the Mitchell-Beazley Encyclopedia (published in America as the Random House Encyclopedia). It was written with the superb assistance and collaboration of Mrs. Greta Fleming Stock.

"Gurdjieff, Ouspensky, and Esoteric Philosophy" was written on the invitation of Professor Robert McDermott and presented at the 1980 national meetings of the American Academy of Religion. It is here published for the first time.

Finally, I wish to express my ever-increasing gratitude to Olivia Byrne who, as always, cheerfully accepted the burden of reading through this manuscript and also, as always, returned with insightful suggestions. First as a pupil, then as my teaching assistant at San Francisco State University, her generous help, far beyond the call of duty, has made many things possible in my own work.

San Francisco
July 1981

WHY PHILOSOPHY IS EASY

In *The Guide for the Perplexed* (Pt. I, Chap. XXXIV) Maimonides explains why the pursuit of metaphysical knowledge is reserved for the very few and why, even for them, it must not begin until they have reached fullest maturity. The subject, he says, is difficult, profound, and dangerous. He who seeks this knowledge, which is equated with wisdom, must first submit to a long and difficult preparation—mental, moral, and physical. Only then can he risk the incomparably more difficult and lengthy ascent to wisdom.

This naturally calls to mind Plato's plan of education in which the highest pursuit, philosophy, is also to be the last in line. With Plato, as with Maimonides, we read that the direct search for wisdom is to be preceded by a certain training of all the natural faculties of man: the body, the emotions, and the intellect.

Note that it is not only wisdom that is so high and so difficult of attainment, and which requires such remarkable preparation. It is also the search for wisdom, the love of wisdom—*philosophy,* properly so-called—which requires this preparation. And so the question arises: how is it that in the modern era philosophy is no longer difficult in this rather special sense? Has something been gained or lost? Are our sights lower or is our aim better?

To this last question, many—perhaps very many—modern thinkers would reply that philosophy has simply freed itself from a certain grandiose illusion, and that in "lowering" its sights it has indeed raised them toward what is possible and realistic. Detached from the goals of religion, practical ethics, and therapy, it seeks primarily to *think well* about problems that are most fundamental in human experience and cognition. The modern philosopher, in his philosophizing, no longer loves, i.e., searches for a condition of the self, a new state of being.

It is the abandonment of this objective, more than any single conceptualized point of view, that distinguishes modern philosophy from so much of ancient and medieval philosophy. When Plato speaks of the realignment of the elemental functions of the soul as the goal of the philosopher, when the ancient Skeptics speak of *ataraxia,* the Stoics of an inner collectedness and "indifference," and, of course, when so many of the medieval philosophers intertwine the aim of their thinking with the aims of the religious process, they are all speaking and thinking in a language that modern philosophy finds unacceptable. To be sure, there are still very many philosophers who approve these goals as such. It is just that we cannot understand or accept that they are to be attained or sought after in our philosophical activity.

In liberating itself from the influence of theology, modern philosophy sought, of course, to rest itself on the touchstone of experience. By and large, every modern philosophical effort ultimately bases itself on the evidence of experience—be it the experience of existentially crucial situations, the experience of perception, the experience of linguistic usage, the experience of moral decisions, the experience of emotions, or the experience of thinking and judging.

It would be belaboring the obvious to spell out this point in great detail. Certainly it is no exaggeration to say that, in this sense, common human experience is the touchstone of almost all modern philosophical thought. Experience is something we all have, and we have only to apply our thought in one way or another to the test of experience to determine the rightness or wrongness of our philosophy. Naturally, there are great problems, great difficulties in definition, communication, the assessment of evidence, the selection of experience, etc. But *in principle* we all have the wherewithal with which to test our philosophy. To say of any system or philosophical position that it does not accord with experience is to condemn it beyond redemption.

How could it be otherwise? Yet, in an enormously important sense, it has been otherwise with philosophy. Indeed, it is this emphasis on and trust in our experience which makes modern philosophy easy. The Platonic philosophy is exemplary of philosophy as *difficult* precisely because the appeal to given experience is never the basis of a line of thought. At most, general human experience is used to exemplify a line of thought whose ultimate purpose is to undermine man's reliance on experience.

In fact, it could be said that for Plato—and for the others in the tradition that takes philosophy to be difficult—man has no experience; or, to put it another way, his experience is not anything like what he imagines it to be. Therefore, the education toward philosophy must involve the acquisition by man of the ability to have genuine experience. The love of wisdom can fully emerge in a man only after he has acquired at least a small degree of this ability. It is, in any case, not something men are born with or which they acquire in the ordinary, general process of maturation and education. Now, what does this mean?

To try to explicate this it will be most helpful here to make use of the Platonic psychology—though one could as well use several other ancient or medieval philosophies. Staying with Plato will enable us to put off until later the highly charged issue of the relationship between philosophy and religion. For the moment, what will be explored is the idea that the quality of the true philosopher's experience stands to common human experience much in the way that what we take to be our common human experience stands to the experience of those we call mad.

Consider for a moment what this would mean if it were true. Why, in the plainest possible sense, do we profoundly distrust the experience of the mentally ill? Though this is neither the time or place to go into the various theories of psychopathology, may we not say that, for whatever reason and in the light of whatever psychological theory we adopt, the perceptions and judgments of the mentally ill are to an extraordinary degree ruled by certain powerful fears or desires, of which they are not aware? This is surely the primary element we have in mind when we say of the psychotic that he cannot see reality, that he lives in a dream or nightmare, that he is the slave of his subjectivity, etc.

The mentally ill may, and very often do, think about philosophical problems. In fact, speaking quantitatively of course, there is more philosophical activity on many mental wards than is to be found even in our academic departments of philosophy. Thought, and even systems of thought about the nature of reality, the existence of God, the mind-body problem, the problem of other minds, the concept of goodness, the reality of evil, can be found there in great abundance. And no one who has ever had extensive first-hand acquaintance with the mentally ill will tell you their thought lacks logical consistency and systematic coherence. Of course, their philosophy is bad because their experience is bad. The experience which their philosophy explains is bad experience. And, again, the reason it is bad experience is that their desires and fears govern their power to perceive and judge. For such people philosophy is even easier than it is for us.

For Plato our common human experience is of a similar quality, and his diagnosis of the human condition is, in essential aspects, such as to relegate all men to the insane asylum. As we know, the inner human condition, life in the cave, is described as a state of affairs in which the lower element in man, the multiform desires and fears, rules the higher elements, *thumos* and *nous.* Unregenerate man spends his life as a pawn of these desires and fears (the appetitive element) which themselves do not seek knowledge, but only a sort of gratification much like the scratching of an itch.

This idea of the passive submission to the appetitive is what lies at the basis of Plato's derogation of sensory experience. That is, it is this particular sort of passivity—the very opposite of self-mastery—that characterizes unregenerate man's sensory life. Man's immediate contact with the world is not just through the senses, but also and equally through the appetitive reaction to the data of the senses. Thus it is not that the senses deceive; it is that the appetitive reaction is not in the interest of truth, but only in the interest of its immediate and—with respect to the whole of man—partial gratification.

Even so, man's situation would not be so bad were it not that this passive submission to the appetites extends also to the realm of thought and judgment. For here, too, the thoughts that fly through the mind like birds in an aviary are accepted or rejected according to the likes and dislikes that are sourced in the appetitive element. That is to say, the very same part of man which automatically seeks pleasure and avoids pain with regard to the data of the senses also seeks pleasure and avoids pain with regard to the concepts of the mind. This general state of affairs, or condition of the psyche, is termed *doxa,* opinion. With regard to the senses only, it is called *eikasia,* imagination.

But this is not all. Plato tells us that there is in man a certain power or function—perhaps, in modern terms, a certain emotional force—called *thumos,* "the spirited element" which, serving the desires and fears, locks man even more deeply in his psychic cave. For without the aid of *thumos* the "multitude in the soul" could never have the strength—simply because it is such a "rabble"—to cause man constantly and passionately to trust in and fight for the goals of this multitude. And this, ironically, in the name of victory, conquest, achievement, "hard struggle," devotion, self-realization, or—most ironically—love.

So that, with *thumos* thus serving the appetites, the force that could help turn the psyche toward genuine freedom and self-mastery plunges man into the darkness of the double lie or veritable lie, a state of inner deception in which falsehood is passionately and proudly held fast. As Cushman has observed,[1] here lies the source of *hubris,* false pride: the misdirected *dunamis* of the "spirited element" in its attachment to the multiform and inconstant appetitive element. In modern terms it might be possible to speak of this as the origin of the "ego."

If experience is understood to be that which happens to us, it is clear that from the above perspective all that happens to us—or, rather, in us—is the satisfaction or dissatisfaction of our appetites. In a way, *nothing* happens to us, to *me*, but only to "the multitude in the soul." In such a case, truth becomes that which satisfies one or another of this multitude, and the desire for truth becomes the desire to master reality, rather than to experience it: the desire to obtain pleasure and avoid pain. And thus the ability to have experience becomes the first goal, rather than the unquestioned assumption, of the seeker of truth.

Clearly, the first step toward this ability is the knowledge of one's own condition of delusion. Presumably, this is the first real experience possible for a man whose inner life is in such chaos. That is, the first real experience is the experience that one has no veridical experience. But where in a man can this experience come from? Certainly not the appetitive element, and certainly not the spirited element. Nor from nor in the thought that serves these elements.

In the Platonic psychology real experience can be obtained only through the functioning of the highest element in the psyche, *nous*. Now, the state in which this element can function uninfluenced by the other elements is called *wisdom*. Thus, to realize one's own inability to experience already requires the active functioning of that which *can* experience. And thus, on strictly psychodynamic and structural terms, the Delphic Oracle is vindicated: Socrates *is* wise in knowing his ignorance. Wisdom is a state of being, a condition of psychic organization, and has little, if anything, to do with the lodgment in thought of correct propositions about the universe, man, or even oneself.

Until this reorganization of the psyche has begun to take place, until the experience of certainty—which is sourced only in the active functioning of *nous*—has been touched, philosophical speculation may be anything but a help toward the attainment of wisdom. For the very idea of what knowledge is and the purposes it may serve is, in unregenerate man, a direct or distant product of his desires and fears. And what he therefore achieves when he achieves satisfying explanations or criticism is to become that much more fixed in the condition of the psyche termed *opinion*.

The search for wisdom—*philo-sophia*—requires, therefore, a uniquely extensive preparation and is the proximal goal of education. Philosophy is thus, in this sense, not a part of education, but its first end-purpose. If philosophical speculation is presented or given to the appetites, which have their own utilitarian manner of thinking, it may lead to the illusion that wisdom or the ability to know is already present in a man when in fact he may have never had the real experience of certainty about anything, himself or the universe; and if by chance he has experienced it, this experience will have been used and distorted by the appetites. The whole body of Plato's pedagogical prescriptions may be understood as part of a method that would lead a sufficiently interested man toward this sense of philosophy.

For the philosopher, to know is to experience *via* the activity of the *nous*. And so the age-old philosophical questions become for him directives for possible experiencing. But unregenerate man approaches philosophical knowledge as propositional and deductive—and based, of course, on his now questionable experience. To put it another way, the philosopher seeks in the act of thinking to embody with the whole of his psyche the structure of reality. This is, perhaps, the primal sense of the activity of reflection and speculation: a psychodynamic mirroring of the structure of reality. Such a task requires consciousness and, ultimately, control of the appetites which, for their part and in their moment, bring with them standards of satisfaction not necessarily congruent with the laws of the universe. By struggling against a passive submission to the appetitive element, the philosopher in the act of reflecting seeks to incarnate the functional and structural order of the universe.

Obviously, such a goal if accepted prematurely could easily lead to the most preposterous sort of self-inflation, and it is for this reason, among others, that the study of metaphysics is so dangerous. Only a man who has experienced the nullity of his ordinary experience—such as a Socrates—and who can therefore be more or less persistently watchful of himself, could seriously undertake the study of metaphysics, i.e., the perfection of wisdom that leads to a man's inner life mirroring the *entire* scale of cosmic order.

Logical-deductive thought in itself, *dianoia,* may be a useful aid in giving the pupil a taste, so to say, of an activity uninfluenced by the appetites. But precisely because it is removed from the lower elements, it is blind to them. As an activity of the psyche, it requires a severing of parts, not a mastery of the lower by the higher. It requires concentration, a philosophical withdrawal, and cannot, therefore, as an activity, mirror an organic cosmic order. It can serve *any* cognitive purpose and in the hands of an ordinary man it can maintain him in his ignorance—at any point blithely withstanding the test of "experience" and allowing him to move on, unchecked, to consistency and systematic error.

I believe there is a widespread misconception about the roots of Western philosophy. It is often said that Eastern thought differs radically from the mainstream of Western thought in that it does not separate philosophy and religion. That is, there are many who believe that only in the East is the effort to think about the nature of reality inextricably bound up with the project of transforming the nature of man. Certainly this is true of the way Eastern thought differs from modern Western philosophy, by which I mean philosophy since the scientific revolution. And perhaps this is why there has recently been a growing interest in various Eastern philosophies: Buddhism in its several forms, Vedanta, Taoism, etc. But by identifying the whole of Western philosophy with the temper of modern philosophy, one may well read this temper into much of ancient and medieval philosophy. One may fail to sense that its form and method may have been an attempt at a practical embodiment of its discursive content, and that its deepest purpose was, perhaps, to awaken in the listener or reader the beginnings of a hunger for wisdom in the sense we have described. One may fail to sense this even while spending one's life espousing its content. Just as modern philosophy is easy, so it has, perhaps, become easy to read the ancients.

The separation of the goals of philosophy from the goals of religion may therefore be a typically modern, rather than a typically Western phenomenon. If so, if there is a way of understanding philosophy and religion as tending toward a common goal, then some interesting questions also arise about the modern Western understanding of religion. Is the attainment of wisdom the goal of the religious process? Did Western religion itself change in such a way as to encourage the philosopher to be quite sure he could think more reliably, and ultimately guide his life, without its help? Did it, too, fall away from its primary goals? Finally, was Western philosophy once a religious way, or an essential part of a religious way?

This last question may be, if not answered, at least approached by attempting to place religion as it is known to us in the perspective of our discussion of Platonic wisdom. To do this it will be helpful to expand upon a certain well-known simile concerning the ultimate unity of the various religions of the world:

One often comes across the idea that the various religions are to each other like the spokes of a wheel in that they emanate from a common center; therefore, as one comes to understand any one religion one comes to understand all religion. Let us assume that this center is the state of being or realignment of psychic functions which Plato and others have called wisdom. And let us assume that, with respect to individual men, it is the ultimate task of religion to bring man from his ordinary psychological condition to this state of wisdom.

It may already seem that we are begging the question by assuming this to be the ultimate goal of religion. But, among the things this simile is designed to illustrate is both the particular difficulty of deciding such an issue, and the fact that this extraordinary difficulty is no argument against there actually being a goal that is common to all genuine religion.

Our simile shall be geographical; we locate the center at some point on the surface of the earth, say the top of a particular mountain. Instead of spokes, we shall speak of paths or routes proceeding from a number of locations quite distant both from each other and from the mountain, and which therefore exhibit great differences with respect to climate, terrain, social and biological conditions, and so forth. One path proceeds from the tropics, another from the polar regions, another from the desert, another from a large city. We shall further assume that, compared to conditions on the mountain, the state of wisdom, these other places are bad places: the desert is dry and barren; the jungle dangerous; the arctic cold and isolated; the cities crowded and artificial, and so forth. It is therefore the ultimate task of religion to enable the inhabitants of these places to find their way to the mountain. To this end, certain sets of directions, handbooks, maps, practical advice, and—most important— guides are made available to the various inhabitants.

Thus, the farther away from the mountain, the greater will be the difference in the travel advice. Those starting from the desert, for example, might be told "Thou shalt carry great quantities of water," something that might be unnecessary and even a hindrance to those proceeding from the jungle. And the prescription to wear warm clothing would be disastrous to both these groups, whereas it would be a vital necessity to those starting in the polar regions.

A crucial element in this interpretation of religion is already apparent—namely, that the primal significance of religious forms (and imperatives) is their *instrumentality,* that their root function is to serve as a means toward psychological transformation. Now, obviously, an effective set of instructions for traveling through a particular region must be based on solid knowledge about the terrain, its dangers, its problems, etc. So that, *for someone who does not wish to leave the region,* these instructions could be taken as ways to improve his life *in* the region. Obviously, much of what would help us travel *out* of the desert could also serve to make life *in* the desert easier or more efficient, *thus reinforcing our satisfaction with where we are.*

There are many ways in which this state of affairs can be translated into the problems of this essay. One that immediately springs to mind is the taking of instrumental formulations as *dogma,* in the modern, pejorative sense of the term. Another possible translation would be the taking of a set of ideas designed to help us change our orientation toward the quality of our experience of the universe as themselves finalistic explanations of that experience. In short, *theology.*

What is being suggested here as a possibility is that dogmatic theology, as we generally understand it, is an instance of transforming the instrumental into the finalistic. An identical situation exists as a possibility with regard to what are termed the moral imperatives of religion. "Thou shalt carry water" is an imperative only as long as we are in dry places. But if we wish to stay in the desert it becomes an absolute imperative and thereby ceases to work as a help toward bringing us out of the desert.

Let us say that it is this form or stage of religion that modern philosophy rejected. By identifying this level of religion with religion as such it unwittingly lost the possibility of moving beyond that level. For, philosophy's rejection is based, in part, on the idea that it can improve upon the explanations of dogmatic theology. And, in a certain limited sense, perhaps it can. But by seeking only to do better what dogmatic theology seemed to do, it fixes itself at what is only an early way-station on the path to wisdom—even, perhaps, while using the word "wisdom" to express its goal. Thus, there may be even more efficient ways of living well in the desert.

Consequently, philosophy, while detaching itself in this way from a relatively elementary form of religion, remains itself—with regard to the actual attainment of wisdom—forever bogged down on that same elementary level. No matter how intricate, subtle, or comprehensive its thought becomes, it will never move from that level. And thus, when an even more efficient way of living in the desert comes along—Western natural science—it is quick to recognize this as its master, or at least as that to which it must direct most of its energies. From the point of view of the actual attainment of wisdom, the development of philosophy from Descartes through Locke, Hume, Kant, and the contemporary schools thus represents little more than the rationalization of the chains that hold man in the cave. Philosophy becomes easy.

Our simile can be used to express several other things about the religions of the world. For example, to many people one of the most repugnant aspects of some religions is their claim to exclusiveness and the concomitant condemnation of other religions. But if we take this as instrumental, it can become more understandable. If we are living in the desert, then only a certain limited set of directions can help us get out of the desert. To follow an arctic handbook would kill us. Or, seen from another angle, if one considers the psychological and environmental conditions of a certain period and place, the most *useful* imperative might well involve the necessity of submission to some form of authority.

In other conditions, or at a certain point along the way—say, when we are safely out of the desert—it may be more *useful* to us (as judged by the guide) to try to understand that there are other paths as well. In any event, as the paths get closer to the center, the terrain naturally becomes more and more similar for everyone no matter from whence they started; therefore, the various sets of directions become more alike until, finally, they are all mountain-climbing directions, differing only with respect to the face of the mountain that is being scaled. It is only as one climbs the mountain, however, that one can actually *see* some of the other paths and the people traveling them; only then can one actually verify that the various religions lead to a common center.

Thus, the question as to whether the state of wisdom is the end-purpose of the religious cannot really be decided until one is rather far along towards wisdom. Otherwise, it would mean placing our trust in that quality of experience which it is the first lesson of wisdom to distrust. Consequently, there is no neutral ground upon which to stand in judging either the goals of the religious ways or in comparing the ways themselves. "Neutral ground" in this case would mean to be on no path at all, i.e., the darkest part of the cave (and, incidentally, the place where philosophy is easiest).

This now brings us to what is perhaps the most important aspect of our whole problem. For one may very well ask, does all this mean we are to surrender our critical faculties, our philosophical methods, our trust in science and in our own moral sense, abandoning all our present intellectual goods, feeble as they may well be when compared to the ideal of wisdom and self-perfection?

One may well ask this, having heard of such notions as "the crucifixion of reason," "belief by virtue of the absurd," having read of the methods of the Zen Buddhists, and having studied the writings of the great mystics, many of whom seem to exhort us to cast away our rationality, such as it is.

We know, most of us, that we cannot do this. We cannot even wish to do this, not even if we felt able to do so. And not even though we might, somewhere in ourselves, agree that this rationality by itself may never lead us to a certain quality of thought for which we might have hoped in answer to the fundamental life-questions that first brought many of us to the study of philosophy. Even so, we are not able to give it up.

But perhaps to see this fact about ourselves is already to have glimpsed a most crucial aspect of *our* condition here and now, one feature, so to say, of our geographical situation. It would be from here, then, that our movement towards wisdom would have to begin; from *here*, and not from some other starting-place where the sacrifice of the mind is required. Just as, on another path, Kierkegaard sought to make Christianity the most difficult thing in the world, so we philosophers may wish to find a way to help us make philosophy more difficult.

REFERENCES

1. Robert E. Cushman, *Therapeia* (Chapel Hill: University of North Carolina Press, 1958), p. 75.

MAN'S NATURE AND NATURAL MAN

MAN has no nature: this is indeed the great idea of the existentialists. For centuries man has sought to understand himself by searching within for a nature, an essence, a firm structure that determines the scale of his possibilities and, therefore, the direction of his duties and efforts. What am I? What can I become? What ought I to do? Men have approached these primal questions by trying to find their own place within the ordered hierarchy of the created world. We know some of the answers that have been tried: man as spirit, as reason, as will-to-power, as organized matter, as repressed instinct, *etcetera, etcetera*. These, and many more besides, have been understood by various thinkers as expressing man's given essence, that to which he must conform his will or his understanding if he is not to live submerged in delusion or in opposition to his purpose in the universe.

To this the existentialists have answered: in man existence precedes essence, man's essence is to determine his essence, man's nature is to choose his nature, man is condemned to absolute freedom. Of course, common sense wants to reply that certainly there is such a thing as human nature: men seem always to have had the same basic needs, limitations, desires, struggles, hopes, fears. Even the believers in progress will say that what has changed in human history is only man's ability to implement his needs and answer his fears, these needs and fears that he has always had. And certainly those who consider themselves within the Judeo-Christian tradition will speak, as did even Kierkegaard, of man's essential finitude, whereby, as a determinate essence, he is dealt with by higher being and greater freedom.

Furthermore, our Judaism and our Christianity, each in its way, tell us of natural man, man as he is born and as he is before he turns to God in trust or in faith. If man is a being who creates his own nature, what becomes of the idea of natural man? What could religion possibly offer to such a being who, by his very lack of essence, could have nothing added to him, who could have no *needs,* no place to ascend to in an ordered reality, no hope for higher being or greater freedom since he is an existential flux and can never *be,* and since his freedom is, to him, absolute?

What is religion, our Western religion, to say to this existentialist philosophy which, if understood in a certain way, would undermine the whole idea of rebirth and the transformation of human nature that is the soul of Judeo-Christian anthropology? Is there room for existentialism in this religion? And if not, can our religion deny the validity of the real experience of despair and nothingness, the sense of metaphysical and personal vacuum that this philosophy rests upon? To put it in one word: if man has no nature, what can he *hope* for?

In order to think about this question, it will be helpful to have in mind the way the existentialist philosophers have criticized our modern world view, the world view of natural science. We recall that science since Galileo can be understood as a mode of approaching the world in which one aspect of the phenomenal world is given the privileged position of primitive, irreducible fact: the aspect of pure corporeality. The notion of pure corporeality as the reality to which science attends and to which all phenomena are to be reduced is the concomitant of a dictate to the perceiver that he remove himself from the world in order to gain knowledge of what he perceives. The roots of this dictate can be seen most strikingly in the thought of Descartes whose isolation of the realm of consciousness from that of the body and the perceived world leads to this remarkable notion of a pure corporeality which, while devoid of consciousness, is accessible to mathematical knowledge.

If we wish to speak of a basic substance to which all phenomena coming within the sphere of scientific explanation are reduced, it would be this pure corporeality. At the same time, it is important to keep in mind that this concept of pure corporeality is the product of a frame of mind, or attitude, or methodological dictate: namely, to keep the self out of its world as it investigates its world.

This, of course, is the famous Cartesian subject-object split: the sundering of the world into two isolated regions: the *res cogitans,* or thinking substance, the world of consciousness, purpose, *telos,* will, quality, etc., and the *res extensa,* pure extended matter, non-conscious, non-vital, undifferentiated, quantitative. This subject-object split which has, at the hands of the phenomenologists and existentialists, been scourged as the most disastrous event in four centuries of Western thought, was an expression of a new sense of human self-awareness that had been in the air since the Renaissance: the feeling of man's self-sufficiency and the urge to master that which had revealed itself as a radical Other: nature, the universe. The subject-object split, to be sure, furthered man's alienation from his world, but it seemed to give him, at the same time, the means to bridge the separation in action, if not in philosophical comprehension.

It gave man natural science, the modern objective attitude, the scientific method. If it no longer answered the why of the universe because it had stripped *telos* from the encountered world of *res extensa,* it promised a detailed, well-structured answer to how the universe is and what it is by furthering the development of the mathematical disciplines by which the pure, extended, quantitative stuff of the world was to be known. So much of the philosophical confusion and frustration of the past could be avoided by bundling into the capacious subject all the contradictions and contrariness which had hitherto seemed part of the encountered world. Doubt and confusion came about because the subject unwittingly read himself into the mathematically pristine Other which was the object. It worked, this attitude, in science; it satisfied the needs which it itself had furthered and even engendered.

Now, it is our habit in the West to equate the real with what is knowable. And since our ideal of knowledge came to be mathematics, it was not too long before we began to suspect that this self, or subject, since it was not mathematically knowable in any full sense, was not entirely real. At most, it was merely the pale knowing subject, very much a ghost in a universe of blind, purposeless, homogeneous corporeality.

This purely corporeal universe was a reality of mathematically rigorous laws, wholly quantifiable. The essence of a thing, that which made it what it was, or—rather—what the thing really was underneath its appearances, was understood as a piece of pure matter subsumable under this or that particular law, which law itself was a special case of the larger, general, blind, non-conscious mathematical laws that governed reality, the *res extensa, in toto.*

We need not now concern ourselves with separating the genuine Cartesianism from the remnants of medieval essentialism in this picture. The important point is that the existentialists understood by essence the blind, formal, purposeless determinant of an entity's nature. The existentialist revolution consists in asserting over against this the full reality of the free, conscious, vital, purposing self.

For the existentialists, consciousness, mind, is not a strange and unprecedented *thing* whose workings are somewhat more puzzling than those of its neighbor objects, the things of this world. Nor is it, as Descartes held, a distant spectator, alien and sufficient unto itself, moving like a ghost in the earth. For the existentialists, the problem as to how the mind or subject reaches over to the object is a pseudoproblem which results from the gratuitous and erroneous supposition that consciousness can be understood independently, apart from that which it intends or is conscious of. For them, mind and consciousness are to be defined simply *as* this intentionality, this reference-to, this transcendence. Consciousness, mind, is not viewed as something which intends an object; consciousness *is* this intention. It is clear, then, that what the existentialists object to in the so-called subject-object split is not that the subject and the object are treated as different modes of being; indeed, their whole point is that *their radical difference is not seen,* so that they are forced to stand to each other as two alien kinds of objects, but similar in their self-enclosedness and nontranscendence. For the existentialists, consciousness is thoroughly different from its objects, so much so that it has nothing in common with them and is to be defined simply and merely as the referring-to or directedness-toward its objects. Any other essential qualification of consciousness would again objectify it.

So much by way of epistemological background. Now, if man is the being whose existence precedes essence, that is, if he has no essence, several amazing things are true of him. His past does not determine his present; quite the contrary, his present consciousness chooses, indeed creates, the past which will influence him. Nothing of the past binds him to a particular future; at any moment he can and does change his whole life-plan, changes the meaning of the causes that act on him, changes the causes themselves, creates them by acknowledging them. He gives to external reality its most significant coefficients and predicates. Other human beings he constitutes in the same way they constitute him; relationships between people come to be diagnosed as the mutual effort to make an essence, or object, out of another freedom. A man's life is like a ship that can and does constantly change not only its destination, but its flag, its crew, its captain, its origin, and its cargo as it sails through the mathematically structured blind sea of the Cartesian *res extensa.*

This is an ingenious and powerful idea. Look at some of the puzzles that it helps to explain. How is it that the wise men of old never recognized that the unconscious and its repressed sexual desires lie at the basis of human nature? Because in our time, man gave himself an unconscious, man created his own sexually repressed state. Why do Freudians, Jungians, Sullivanians, and others cure their patients with about equal success? Because their patients become Freudianly sick with a Freudian analyst, Jungianly sick with a Jungian, etc. How is it that Marx was right, Hobbes is right, Rousseau is right, Hegel is right, Hume is right—that is, how is it that they all do a satisfying job of explaining human nature? Because all—not one—of them are right. Man makes himself a creature now of economic forces, now biological, now of hatred and fear, now of habit, and similarly for many, many other forces that exist.

The same is true of the individual. It is not that it is too hard to explain him; it is too easy: he *is* an animal (the idea of which he creates); he *is* a soul (the product of his hopes); he *is* a consequence of his life-history, of his American social mores, of his Puritan upbringing, his climate, his language, his physique, his glands, the size of his sexual organs, the conjunction of his planets, the technological innovations of his century, the transactions of Wall Street, the percentage of acetylcholine in his synapses, the breakfast of his morning, the angry glance of his spouse, the smile of the blonde, the ache of his teeth, the loving kindness of his god, the situation of the Earth in the galaxy . . . he is all of these, not partially, but totally and exclusively. The words are from the Bible, but the idea, understood in this way, is very modern, existentialist: man's name is legion, he has no essence, he determines himself.

But perhaps we should pause a moment. What has happened here? How have we gotten into this remarkable appraisal of man's freedom? And besides, remarkable as it may be, don't we rather find something slightly unbearable about this picture? Is this really a picture of freedom? Somehow, doesn't it smell a bit like slavery? But of this later. Now we want to know how we arrived here. The answer involves a surprising realization: the existentialists, in the energy and single-mindedness with which they battle Cartesianism and scientism, have given away far too much to them. Their denial of Descartes remains a Cartesian denial, they stay strictly within his fold, they are nothing less than Cartesian anti-Cartesians. They give natural science more weight, more credence, more trust than perhaps most scientists themselves do.

To see this, let us return to that ship which is man (individual and collective) sailing tracklessly on that Cartesian ocean. The ocean, pure matter, is deep and dark; it is everywhere the same, it contains no fishes, no plants, no sunken vessels, no islands, no land. All life and all consciousness is in the ship. Some passengers speak about various fishes and whales, some see mermaids, some drop lines hoping to catch something that lives; but the scientists know that at most there are only currents of water, mathematical laws. The passengers, *res cogitans*, the subject, get confused and fancy their images correspond to something dwelling in the lifeless sea. But the oceanologist, our Cartesian, is there to remind them that all purpose, all consciousness, all vital force is in the ship and nowhere else. The most up-to-date scientists among them begin to say that even the passengers are configurations of sea-water. And this is where the existentialist jumps in to defend his rights as a human passenger, denying the very modern scientist's claim that he is dark ocean water governed by the laws of water currents. But, and here is our immediate point, *he never questions the idea that the ocean is empty!*

Our existentialist accepts that blank sea. Indeed, he loves the idea of it every bit as much as the Cartesian. We, as passengers, are very, very different from that sea, the existentialist says. We are not dark and homogeneous and blind. We live, we choose, we create ourselves; we think, we will, we despair, we believe. The sea is reality. Reality is meaningless extension under blind essential laws. We are not this reality; we are alien to it; we are no essence, no thing; we exist as no thing, as nothing, we are consciousness and not matter,—we passengers.

Even if our existentialist is named Heidegger he will tell us that we are radically different beings from that sea, apart from it, alien, going nowhere since all "wheres" are in us, and that our task is to go nowhere resolutely. But whatever his name, our existentialist is a very close friend of the Cartesian; look closely: are they not brothers?

Existentialism has not denied the metaphysics of natural science. It has simply attached what it would consider a more humanistic twist to the metaphysics of natural science. The universe is meaningless; it has no purpose; God is dead; there is no consciousness, no life, anywhere but in man. Man is a purposing being in a purposeless universe, a passenger with a baited hook and line and a busy, sometimes poetic, imagination, crossing a truly dead sea.

Natural science rejected the medieval idea of a hierarchically ordered universe with different levels of being all united in an organic, higher plan. Existentialism rejects it too. Natural science made it fruitless to ask *why* things are the way they are. Existentialism agrees. Natural science denied the idea of an entity's purpose, its place in nature, its function, its good, its possibilities, its task. Existentialism emphasizes that denial by taking it as the cue for despair. Natural science homogenizes all of reality, ignores the possibility of a difference in scale, removes all angels and devils. Existentialism picks through the garbage can of natural science, finds empty copies of these ideas and defiantly reinstates them by inserting them in its lyric heart. (But these sharks, dolphins, barracuda, and other fish do not live on board ship. They live in the ocean.) Natural sci-

ence denies that life is a fundamental property of matter. Grimly, resolutely, the existentialists agree.

There have always been some, however, who saw the close relationship between philosophy and religion—for example, the ancient world
in Plato and in many of his predecessors. These, apparently, were
schools of thought that sought to understand the outer world as they
sought at the same time to understand and transform the inner world.
Thus, the intimate relationship, the identity of knowledge and virtue—
the idea strikes the modern mind as quaint.

Life and purpose were understood as in the core of reality. These philosophers recognized that there must, of necessity, be many, many different kinds of life and different scales of purpose, all of which might seem
strange or even invisible to general humanity. But the conclusion they
drew from this invisibility was not that these purposes did not exist, but
that they must try to look for them in a different way.

We often hear it said that the natural-scientific revolution and its
continuing development have meant the humbling of man, that modern
thought from Galileo through Darwin to Freud and the existentialists
differs dramatically from the ancient and medieval in that it removes
man from his exalted place in the universe. But this is a superficial observation, for the truth is quite the reverse. The root idea of the ancient
and medieval systems was, in this regard, the exaltation of man's *possible*
development and transformation. But modern science exalts man's *actual* natural state. Unable to glimpse the possibilities of inward human
development, it exalts ordinary knowledge, by which is meant the
knowledge that belongs to man in his ordinary or natural state.

The modern world has taken for granted that every man knows the
true from the false, or that everyone has the natural light which he need
only follow to find what is right, or that we need only doubt until we
come to the veridical, or that we need only trust our senses, or think dia-
lectically, or simply look about us. We may find that we are alone, alien,
far off center in a blind vast cosmos, but *we,* we natural men with a natural light, we can discover at least this ultimate fact, this truth that
eluded such poor strugglers as Jesus, Moses, Plato, Pythagoras, and
others who, unfortunately, did not have the telescope, or psychoanalysis,
or phenomenology, or some other marvelous instrument. The kind of
purpose we look for is the only kind of purpose that could exist. If we
cannot find it, no purpose of any sort exists.

What could be less humbling than to think our consciousness is a
strange, ontologically unprecedented kind of reality, so unprecedented
that it is, in the view of some, even *outside* reality: that we are alien to *all*

of reality, that we are apart! Poor consciousness! But like all self-pity, isn't this only a mask that conceals the most extravagant sense of our own importance? Are we not so remarkable, so extraordinary that there is nothing like us in all of reality? We are the subject against an object that is no less than the All. We are alone and lonely: how marvelous, how comforting. If we cannot have what we want, it must be because we are rare, unique. Not even the most naive interpretation of the phrase "made in God's image" ever gave man such an elevated ontological status!

Instead of questioning himself and the way he searches for meaning, natural man believes in his questioning, never doubts that he is living his question in the right way. Even when the conclusions he reaches are as grandiloquently absurd as those of the existentialist-scientist, he accepts them, and with courage. But we must ask what real courage would be in such a case. This, at any rate, is the question put to us by the root teachings of the great religions. The answer that is given, which is no answer in any external sense, is that courage would be to try to understand that we, and not reality, are in the cul-de-sac.

What? Does this mean we are to return to some shopworn, naive idea of natural man, bestial, evil, ontologically fixed, blessed by his maker with an artificial freedom and reason which, if exercised at all, either condemns him to punishment or earns him a bodiless existence in some tedious paradise? Are we to revive a view of human nature that either fails to see man's animality or else buries him in it to such a degree that his consciousness and reason are at best only minor epiphenomena? Finally, and most importantly, are we to deny the fact of man's constant change and fluidity, the constant movement of his consciousness that can at every moment change a whole life-plan even while the cells of the body and neurons in the brain run on in their rigorously determined way? Who can ask us to deny the great idea that man has no essence, and deny with it the experience of nothingness by means of which existentialism has irresistibly defined our age? And if we are not to deny this, what possible basis is there for a religion? How are we to hold on to the idea of natural man while admitting that man has no nature?

By this we are at our thesis: namely, that from the point of view of religion, *natural man has no nature*. It is precisely this teaching that lies at the practical heart of the great religions not only of the West but of the world. Therefore, in a certain crucial sense, the existentialist diagnosis of the human condition poses no threat whatever to the religious idea of natural man. For it is none other than natural man whom the existentialists—to be sure, in their rosy fashion and even then only to a degree—describe as unbound by essential structures, undetermined by anything fixed within, ungoverned by a permanent, inner nature.

But natural man is not free. On the contrary, he is a slave.

From the practical, religious point of view, existentialist man, the man without a nature, is so seemingly unbound only because he is so totally bound by forces acting on him from without. His life is passed, from the moment of birth to the moment of death, merely reacting to external influences. As the influences change, so does he change. His father and mother, the climate, the chemistry of his cells, the smile of the blonde, the scowl of the waiter, the conjunctions of his planets and stars, the laws of physics, the nod of the psychoanalyst, the bad dream, the flattering letter, the good beefsteak, the headlines, the oxygen balance in the air, and much, much else besides, all determine him and each can, in its moment, determine him completely. This last is crucial, for it is no great news to hear that many forces work upon us; almost everyone would agree to that. But what may be new is the idea that any of these influences can, at its given moment, determine the *whole* of me.

The result would be this: at one moment I am one thing, totally; at another moment, I will be something else, *totally*. The next moment, something else. I wish to do one thing, a very good thing. Next moment, I do not wish to do it, it is not good. Next moment I wish I had done it. Next moment I am proud I did not do it. Next moment I forget about it and daydream about dinner. Next moment . . . The existentialist will say that the will changes, that it is bound to nothing. To be sure. But whose will is it? A practical examination of this state of affairs may well reveal that there is no *person,* no *self* that persists underneath or behind these changes. The existentialist might try to claim that there is this self, but he bases this claim at best on the fact that with each change of will there is a faint or strong sense of persistence. At his worst, he argues from some abstract notion of a transcendental ego that solves his problem by definition. When he argues in these two ways he either ignores the possibility that each little self has its own partial and sometimes illusory memory, or—in the latter case—he is simply intellectualizing the delusion of man's unity and perhaps forgetting that he was the one who claimed nothing abiding in human nature.

The existentialist may even go further: he may claim that at any moment I can and do constitute a new self with a differently structured past and future project, with new coefficients of meaning placed upon all my fears and desires. If one would ask him the cause of these changes, he would deny the question any significance. Consciousness, he will say, is that means by which causality enters the world. Therefore, there is no sense in asking what causes it.

There are many things to be said to this, but isn't it clear that the existentialist can maintain such a position only because of a Cartesianism in which the very idea that something may causally influence consciousness violates his whole metaphysics? Only material things, in the sense of *res extensa,* work causally, or can be seen to work causally, or can be structured by the mind within a causal framework. Thought is outside this framework, it sets up the framework: therefore, it is uncaused, acausal. But, from another, non-Cartesian, framework wherein life and purpose, far from being set apart or exceptional are ingrained in the heart of reality—in such a point of view, human thought and feeling and willing would be processes in the same cosmic order that embraces supernovae, chemical reactions, and gravitational forces.

One may, therefore, grant the existentialist the idea that at every moment a new self appears complete with a valorically and factually different memory, with different desires, fears, and thoughts. One may grant him this without coming to his rather flattering conclusion that we are, therefore, radically free. For that conclusion is inescapably bound to a world view in which something called consciousness is understood to exist totally outside the pale of the rest of reality. If we replace that world view with another that sets the processes of thought, desire, and sensation within a vast, ordered whole, then something quite interesting happens: that very same idea of the existentialist ceases to be an expression of man's radical freedom and becomes instead an index of his utter dependence upon external influences. For, in such an ordered whole, freedom would presumably manifest itself not by change, but by permanence, not by the feeling of choice, but by the persistence of will: purity of heart, to will one thing in time.

Suppose we attempt to abandon the metaphysics that underlies existentialist scientism, and suppose we attempt to see the universe more as Plato suggested, as an organic whole in which every entity influences and is influenced by every other entity within a frame of varying scales of purpose, structure, and time. Then the existentialist evaluation of the idea that man's existence precedes his essence begins to suggest this state of affairs: a little boy, pale and perhaps sickly, is unable to play with the gang of older, tougher boys who scornfully ignore him. This pale little boy sits himself in a tree and every time something happens in the older boys' games he shouts, "I made you do that! You did just what I wanted!"

The little boy would be man's consciousness, that in a man which says "I." The big boys would be the processes of body, emotion, sensation, and, perhaps, also thought. No matter what happens, even if the big boys begin to get angry and throw stones at him, the pale little boy says, "I'm causing you to do that!" Often, this little boy has another kind of dream: when something wonderful happens on the field, he imagines it is he who did it; sometimes he has a nightmare: when something terrible happens to him, he imagines it is he who caused it. This "I" of natural man, palest of all existences, most subject to outer influences (that exist both in his organism and in the universe), most inconstant, dreams that he is king of himself.

We may also remark in passing that, obviously, if this is natural man, it would be an even grosser lie to single out one or two of these myriad influences as the sole moving force of human behavior. This is the error of the determinism and reductionism that is rightly rejected by the existentialists. Forgetting for now the question as to whether even these few influences are properly understood by the reductionists, it is clear that this arbitrary partiality for certain kinds of influences leads to naive notions of man as an animal as a product of environment, of physiology, economics, climate, divine spirit, and so forth. This can well be understood as the basic meaning of essentialism as it applies to man, and if put in this way, necessarily must be rejected.

Plato, describing the condition of natural man, also uses the image of a ship:

> Imagine this state of affairs on board a ship or a number of ships. . . . The sailors are quarrelling over the control of the helm; each thinks he ought to be steering the vessel, though he has never learnt navigation and cannot point to any teacher under whom he has served his apprenticeship; what is more, they assert that navigation is a thing that cannot be taught at all, and are ready to tear in pieces anyone who says it can. Meanwhile they besiege the master himself, begging him urgently to trust them with the helm; and sometimes, when others have been more successful in gaining his ear, they kill them or throw them overboard, and, after somehow stupefying the worthy master with strong drink or an opiate, take control of the ship, make free with its stores, and turn the voyage, as might be expected of such a crew, into a drunken carousel. (*Republic,* 488, Cornford)

This is a picture of the inner condition of natural man: there is no permanent presence or self. It is drugged, imprisoned. And each of the little selves in turn grabs after the helm, steers according to its impulse or fear, and in the brief span of its captaincy says "I." But we know the general course of this ship: it will follow the currents and the winds. Each moment one sailor wrests the helm from the hands of another, and each momentary helmsman feels free to do as he likes. Let us imagine that this is a large crew with hundreds, perhaps thousands, of sailors of very different types, some perhaps in groups, some physically stronger than others. Each has his turn, is thrown down, or swoons, and in the course of the voyage takes his opportunity again and again to grab the wheel, depending on a multitude of chance factors.

What is the essence of this ship? We are compelled to answer that it has no essence. Or, what comes to the same thing, that its essence is multiplicity and flux. To be even more precise: its essence, which we might take as symbolized by the captain, is drugged. It may be there, but instead of ruling, it is ruled, overpowered, if not murdered, by what was meant to serve, symbolized by the sailors. To establish the inner republic of man of which Plato speaks would involve some practical means of getting the captain and sailors back where they belong. Thus, we arrive at the idea of religion and its work.*

It is interesting that existentialism is understood as deriving from the thought of Kierkegaard. Kierkegaard's concern with religion is taken as separable from his existential thinking. This latter is then singled out as his great discovery, and such terms as dread, despair, anxiety, leap, and so forth, are abstracted from his relationship to Christianity. They are interpreted as universally human categories, understandable outside the religious context, and *subsequently* they may or may not serve religious thinking, depending on the interests of the particular existentialist philosopher who uses them.

But after all that has been discussed, the relationship between Kierkegaard and the existentialists will appear very different. And why it does may throw some light on the work of religion vis-à-vis natural man.

The Sickness Unto Death begins:

> Man is spirit. But what is spirit? Spirit is the self. But what is the self? The self is a relation which relates itself to its own self . . . the self is not the relation but that the relation relates itself to its own self. Man is a synthesis of the infinite and the finite, of the temporal and the eternal,

---

* This is not the place for a discussion of the difference between religion and psychotherapy. We may simply suggest that psychiatry as a natural science knows only natural man. Looking at this ship, natural science has no idea that there is a captain locked up somewhere. It worries only that there is too much strife in the ship. But, of course, even if this were a happy ship, we would have to ask, from the standpoint of the work of religion: where is this ship going? what is its Good? This issue is discussed in "Psychiatry and the Sacred" in this volume.

of freedom and necessity, in short it is a synthesis. A synthesis is a relation between two factors. So regarded, man is not yet a self.[1]

And, in *The Concept of Dread*:

> But the possibility of freedom does not consist in being able to choose
> the good or the evil. Such thoughtlessness has as little support in the
> Scripture as in philosophy. Possibility means *I can*. In a logical system it
> is convenient enough to say that possibility passes over into actuality. In
> reality it is not so easy, and an intermediate determinant is necessary.
> This intermediate determinant is dread . . . Dread is not a determinant
> of necessity, but neither is it of freedom; it is a trammeled freedom . . .[2]

There are two main points for us to notice here. First, Kierkegaard
tells us that man is not yet a self. Second, that freedom is power, an able-
ness that man does not yet have. The work of religion in natural man is
to lead him to the acquisition of a self (or soul) and the attainment of
freedom. Everything that Kierkegaard has written is from the point of
view of natural man's possibility of developing in this way. His famous
attack on philosophical thought, for example, is to express the illusion it
can create of the thinker's having attained by mere thought what must
be struggled for in the course of a man's own personal existence. What
has been called Kierkegaard's existential style is the form of writings
that have their real significance only to men who have begun to sense
that they do not yet exist. Furthermore, for Kierkegaard, natural man
cannot transform himself and cannot see his own nothingness without
submission to something higher.

But nobody believes Kierkegaard, least of all the existentialist philosophers.
When the religious aspect of Kierkegaard is separated from the rest of
his thought, the rest of his thought evaporates into nothing. What one
loses is the idea of man's *possible* transformation with the help of religion,
and it is this idea which defines *all* aspects of his writings. At the hands
of the existentialists, Kierkegaard's idea of man's possible freedom is
changed into an idea of man's actual freedom. Once this quick-change is
made, all idea of help becomes superfluous and existentialism becomes
philosophical talk about passion, desire, will, freedom, *etcetera,* rather
than an effort at a language concerning the transformation of natural
man. No one, therefore, has misunderstood Kierkegaard more than the
existentialists.

Clearly, the modern existentialists do not believe what they themselves say. We read in their books and between their lines that man faces
an abyss, that there is nothing for him to rely in himself, the world, or

above the world, that he is his own law, doomed to nothingness in life and death. But we have seen the existentialists' deep trust in Descartes and natural science to set the reality of their problem, and we have seen that, above all, they trust themselves, their thought, their passions, their hopes and fears to lead them truly. In a word, they trust in natural man, they rely on him even as they argue that he has no essence.

But if we are to believe Kierkegaard, it is the practical work of religion to make it possible for natural man truly to experience his own nothingness, his own lack of being. The new man who will appear in the place of natural man will, indeed, have a nature, an essence, an existence of his own. But for this to occur, man may need the help of a religion to see his natural man for what it is. And what it is may be an even more surprising nothingness than the existentialists describe.

In the end, our question may simply become Kierkegaard's: What kind of religion? What it will do? How will we recognize it? Is it here in front of us? How should we look for it?

REFERENCES

1. Sören A. Kierkegaard, *The Sickness Unto Death* (Princeton: Princeton University Press, 1941), p. 17.
2. Sören A. Kierkegaard, *The Concept of Dread* (Princeton: Princeton University Press, 1946), pp. 44–45.

NOTES ON RELIGION

Religion: The Nature of Sacred Tradition

The question "What is religion?" has suddenly become of intense concern to many modern people, especially among the younger generation. But it is no longer enough to answer this question by hunting for a conceptual generalization. The academic effort to arrive at a single satisfactory definition of religion is bound to fail not because there is no common essence to all the great religions of the world, but because the practices and teachings of the various religions have in the recent past been examined with the part of mind that divides and analyzes, rather than with the hidden part of mind that can perceive, through its own need, the unity which underlies an outer diversity.

For a contemporary individual, searching not for a new conceptual definition of religion, but for the secret of how to live, the fundamental message of the religious traditions is that *man does not know himself.* He knows neither the extent of his weaknesses nor the possibilities of his greatness. Thus, at the heart of all the sacred traditions of the world there have existed methods and practices by which man can become directly acquainted with *both* the animal and the divinity within him. The early Christian, for example, meditating in the deserts of North Africa and practicing the particularly Christian method of continuous inner prayer (prayer of the heart) directly experiences the enormous extent to which his mind is distracted and filled with illusions about himself. At the same time, facing and accepting this, he also discovers that he is the vehicle for the highest or most divine energies of the universe.

The word "method" must not be misunderstood to mean a mere manipulative technique. Method includes all the forms and ways by which tradition guides human beings as they face the demands of survival, the social and physical needs of everyday life, the fact of death, and the innumerable joys and sorrows of human life on earth. But when used wrongly, as a manipulative device to gratify egoistic aims, all such methods and practices lose their real religious purpose. Thus, the prophets of Israel condemned even the most sacred rituals when they were performed externally without the inner recognition of one's own helplessness and obligation to the source of life. Thus, too, the powerful meditative practices of Mahayana Buddhism, to take an example from Eastern traditions, are said to have a liberating effect only when used with the aim of benefiting all sentient beings.

In its most intensive forms, religion offers even more than that extraordinary knowledge of two opposing natures. When carried far enough, the practices of a great tradition are intended to bring about an actual transformation of human nature at the deepest, causal level. The name given to this state of transformed being varies from tradition to tradition, and also as one or another gradation or aspect of transformation is referred to. In the Western world it is spoken of as salvation, immortality, the attainment of the kingdom of God, among other terms. In the East it is nirvana, liberation, enlightenment, or God-consciousness. Often the terms "wisdom" or "freedom" are used. But whatever the terminology, and whatever the aspect of transformation, it is here, around the idea of transformation, that one may look for the common factor in all the religions of mankind.

A metaphor often employed to express this common aim of all authentic spiritual traditions is that of a mountain with many paths leading to the summit. What is this mountain summit, this state of transformed being that is the common aim of all religions? As we shall see in the following accounts, the possibilities of human development envisaged by religious tradition are very great indeed. Man is understood as a potential *microcosm,* a being who contains in himself all the forces of creation and destruction that operate in the great universe. This concept of the microcosm forms the backbone of all ancient teachings, Eastern and Western, including so-called primitive religions.

The traditional teachings see the misery and confusion of human life as rooted in man's failure to see, accept, and live by the universal order of reality that is contained within himself and within the whole of the universe. In man's "fallen" state, the divinity within him is completely cut off from the animal. Thus divided within himself, man lives his life governed by impulses which were meant to be servants rather than masters. These false masters within man are the *desires,* which are condemned not as such, but only because man wrongly identifies himself with them and obeys them blindly and uncomprehendingly. To become a microcosm, that is, a mirror of the whole reach of the divine, cosmic order, there must be forged within human nature a right relationship between the desires and the slumbering spiritual power with which all are born.

The transformation of man (called the "second birth" in the Christian tradition) consists of the tangible establishment within the self of this right relationship, this extraordinary inner unity. Thus transformed, man may take his central place within the whole scheme of creation. He is then the Great King of the Chinese tradition, the Cosmic Man of Hinduism, The All-Containing Void of Buddhism, or image of God of Judaism and Christianity. He both reflects the whole of cosmic nature and becomes the conscious instrument of the creator within that universal order.

In a very general sense, the ideas, symbols, and rituals of the traditions are meant to serve as instruments to help man experience what is taken to be his exalted cosmic destiny, both on an individual and social level. Thus, the ancient structures of society—what is called theocracy—were established to conform human life to a cosmic pattern which is not perceivable under modern, scientific categories. Teachings about life after death, the animistic view of nature (the belief that all things are filled with life and consciousness), the role of the shaman and the priest, the symbols of so-called polytheism, and the function of magic may all be approached and studied from this point of view, rather than from the conventional perspective which sees them as expressions of intellectually inferior cultures. It is especially revealing to study the awesome social order of ancient Indian and pharaonic Egypt on this basis.

Authentic sacred tradition, whether Eastern or Western in origin, whether primitive or higher, polytheistic or monotheistic, may therefore be defined as a means of transmitting ideas and ways of living which can guide individuals to pierce through the illusions that have become second nature to them and to realize in fact, and not just in fantasy, both the terrors of our present situation and the greatness of our possible inner evolution.

Religion East and West: God Within and God Above

JUDAISM

The fundamental message of Judaism is expressed by a prayer: "Hear, O Israel, the Lord our God, the Lord is One." This prayer is called by its first word—*Sh'ma* ("Listen," "hear," "understand," "obey"). It calls men to hear the truth that has been revealed, to take it to heart, and to live by it in order to realize the unity of God in a relationship which demands of a man that he unify his own being.

Judaism is the religion of the covenant between YHWH (God) and the descendants of Abraham. From the covenant radiates the mystery of an *agreement* between man and God. It is in the actions, in the *history* of the chosen people trying their ways in response to the covenant that the teachings of the Jewish faith are set forth. The Lord appears in all the transcendence of his absolute power and at the same time in the immediacy of personal concern for his people. For man, who is unable to conceive of the Creator as he is in himself, God appears as the deliverer from bondage, bringing Israel out of slavery in Egypt and into the promised land.

The Hebrews are bound by covenant to obey the Lord, and the laws given to Moses are a blessing in response to their need rather than a price to be paid. Israel is chosen, not as those elected for salvation, but as the people of a promise which conveys both hope and responsibility. Far from relieving them of their burdens, God charges his people with a great task: "Ye shall be holy, for I the Lord your God am holy."

For the Jew, the act of his people's being chosen parallels the mystery of creation in God's image. Man is called to fulfill the promise of his being, as Israel is called to realize its covenant. This applies as well to each individual human being considered as a microcosm. Pharaoh and Egypt exist within ourselves.

In Jewish mysticism, the symbolism of exile and return finds yet another level of interpretation, this time on a cosmic scale. Medieval Kabbalists, interpreters of the Torah and its rabbinical commentaries, saw in the failure and exile of cosmic man—*Adam Kadmon*—the scattering of the sparks of the divine *Shekhinah,* the presence of God in the whole of creation. The redemption of man is thus intimately bound up with the redemption of creation.

This conception of man as responsible for the whole of creation had its greatest modern influence on Judaism in the communities of Hasidim ("the pious") that arose in Poland in the eighteenth century. In the Hasidic way of life, there is no separation between sacred and profane. Everything that exists contains within it a divine spark waiting to be liberated. According to this teaching, there is in man a divine energy through which the sparks *everywhere present* can be attracted and set free. All depends on intention, the condition of a man turned to God with his whole being. For the Hasid trying to unite the whole of himself in this turning, everything he meets in the course of his day is holy, and through his actions everything can be brought back to union with God.

CHRISTIANITY

The whole of Christian religion is centered upon the mystery of divine love, and man's task is to respond to that love. From the very source of Christianity come the words of Jesus addressed to the Jews in terms of their own tradition: "Thou shalt love the Lord thy God with all thy heart, and with all thy soul, and with all thy mind. This is the first and great commandment. And the second is like unto it, Thou shalt love thy neighbor as thyself. On these two commandments hang all the law and the prophets" (Matt. 22:37–40).

Later, the Christian faith came to include people who lacked the common basis of Judaism. In response to their need and in the face of the claims of the then current systems of thought, Christianity began to develop its unique perspective and to take shape as an independent religion.

Everything that exists was brought into being as an expression of divine love and is moved by that love to be what it is, to fulfill its own nature as the plant reveals the secret contained in the seed. But in the order of creation, it is man, made in the image of God, who stands out as the element of uncertainty, the great risk freely undertaken by God so that God's love might be freely returned.

In Adam's fall, the limited and separate existence of the natural world apart from its creator asserted itself. Yet this failure is sometimes called "the happy fault" because it was the occasion of the greatest act of divine love. The father's sacrifice of his son, from which Abraham was released, was fulfilled in a *new covenant*. The son of God became man. In the person of Christ, the way was reopened. In Christ, the two natures— human and divine—were united mysteriously in the incarnation, and this unification was demonstrated in the perfect submission of human will to divine will in the passion and death of Jesus. Finally the resurrection of Christ promises the fruit of sacrifice, the new man in whom limited nature is transformed by divine life: "Unless the grain of wheat falling into the ground dies, itself alone remains; but if it dies it brings forth much fruit" (John 12:24). And again: "He that findeth his life shall lose it; and he that loseth his life for my sake shall find it" (Matt. 10:39).

A deep and serious response to this call can be found in the Christian contemplative tradition. In the modern person the idea of contemplation may call forth associations of daydreaming or sentimental ramblings. This is far from the contemplative's understanding of his work and its demand for a quality of awareness and impassioned searching that can bring him to the core of his being, there to discover his true need for God: "For he is your being."[1] Confused and alienated as a result

of the fall, man must struggle to discover the central impulse of love that
calls him to be what he is.

ISLAM

Islam, the youngest of the Western religions, sounds again the message
of God's unity. This time the highest truth takes the form of a denial of
error: "There is no god but God." Recognition of this truth constitutes
the act of submission by which man becomes a Muslim, "one who sub-
mits." Conscious of his dependence, man acknowledges "*I* am not the
absolute." Yet one who is called to the inner path of Islam follows the
same truth to the ultimate realization "I am nothing separate from or
other than the absolute." From this point of view, unity is reflected
everywhere, drawing itself out like a beautiful arabesque that baffles the
eye as it continually turns back on itself to create forms by its own inter-
weaving:

> Since the Lord is thy Origin, thou hast not come; since the Lord is thy
> Goal, thou wilt not go. "There is no God save Allah." Nothing can be
> separated from the Infinite, and attached to non-God. Since the Origin
> is from Him, the end is verily in Him. Separation and union, coming
> and going, are thus unreal.[2]

This is the meaning of divine unity from the perspective of a Sufi, one
who has reached the goal of Islam's inner way. The truth looks very different to those who feel separated from their source. However, the Sufi's
declaration is profound evidence that in Islam the teaching of divine
unity does not mean simply that there is only one God rather than several. It is the key that opens the meaning of creation as a revelation of
the absolute through his divine names or qualities like white light dif-
fused through a prism. As microcosm, man has gathered into himself all
the attributes reflected separately by the other creatures. As one who is
made in the image of God, his greatest potential is, by analogy, to re-
unite all the colors of the spectrum into a spark of divine light. Then it
can be said, "He who knows himself knows his Lord."

According to the Islamic perspective, man is in need of divine revelation to remind him of the one reality which is never *directly* manifested in
the world. Judaism and Christianity are recognized as founded on authentic revelations, and Islam, which traces its descent through Abraham's son Ishmael, is said to offer the third and final revelation.

Mohammed, the "seal of the prophets," was born in Mecca in A.D.
570. He began to fulfill his prophetic function by denouncing the pre-
vailing Arab practice of worshiping many gods. Confronted by powerful

opposition, Mohammed and his followers became a social and political as well as a spiritual force. In keeping with the growth of Islam, the teaching given through Mohammed in the Koran developed both the external and internal aspects of religion, providing laws for the guidance of a religiously oriented community as well as a way for the individual to unite with God.

The outer aspect of Islam engaged all Muslims in definite observances that regulate and harmonize all aspects of life. To be a Muslim means not so much to profess adherence to this or that doctrine as to follow the law in obedience to the will of Allah.

HINDUISM

For the Westerner whose notion of religion is based on the great monotheistic creeds, the religion of India may be a puzzling phenomenon. In place of God and creation, he will find that reality is utterly impersonal and the phenomenal world is ultimately unreal. The search for a charismatic founder will bring him to the edge of human history. Even the idea of history is overshadowed by the sense of a cyclic world drama of creation, preservation, and destruction. Looking for clearly defined doctrines, he is instead plunged into an assortment of methods and beliefs ranging from devotional practices that have no appeal for him emotionally to metaphysical formulas that make no sense to him intellectually.

Yet Hinduism is of interest not only because its ancient truths match the experiential wisdom of Western mystics or because its traditional methods are being popularized in the West but also because of what supports its confusing diversity. In Hinduism, the human side of tradition has been based on inclusion rather than exclusion. A Hindu, devoted to the Divine Mother, tells the whole story: "Mother said to me, 'What, even if unbelievers should enter My temples, and defile My images.' What is that to you? Do you protect Me? Or do I protect you?" In Western traditions, men have done their best to protect the truth from distortion. In Hinduism the truth is left to protect itself.

The simplest—and therefore most difficult—expression of the truth of Hinduism is "Thou art That," which may be understood as a response to the deepest question that man can ask. Historically, the question seems to take two forms. Looking at the world around them, men saw in the sudden flash of lightning, in the invisible power of the wind, signs of energies beyond their control and beyond their understanding. Everywhere there is movement, change. What is the source from which it comes and the end toward which it goes? What is behind all this? The other form of the question was concerned with the mystery within man: I was a child; now I am a man. I was asleep; now I am awake. Where did I come from and where am I going? Who am I? In a single moment of discovery came the answer to both lines of questioning: the true self, the indefinable Atman, is the same as the ultimate ground of reality, Brahman: "Thou art That."

Thus, the Hindu revelation is not the focus of an historical event like the revelation given to Moses. It does not mark a unique bridging of the gap between God and man like the incarnation of Christ. It is only this—the truth is in each person waiting to be realized. With this promise comes the warning *"neti, neti,"* "not this, not that." One cannot identify Atman or Brahman with any particular thing. The self in all things can be known only by an awakening. Until then belief in a separate little self or ego is like an assumed identity that keeps one from realizing one's true self.

BUDDHISM

In many of its forms, Hinduism responds to man's self-delusion like a wise mother who offers her wisdom knowing that some childish dreams will have to be tried and relinquished before it can help. In contrast to this, the teaching of Buddhism is always urgent and direct. It sees ordinary existence as a nightmare which is not less painful because its threats are unreal.

In the sixth century B.C. Gautama Siddhartha, the son of an Indian king, woke from the nightmare. As Buddha ("the awakened") he was forever released from suffering and full of compassion for those who were still in darkness. He taught that suffering is a universal fact of existence because of man's fundamental ignorance about himself and the world. The world is a process of continuous interaction of unstable compounds in which nothing lasts. Whatever a man may take to be himself—body, mind, feeling, perception—is also subject to change. In the midst of this process, man intrudes an obstacle in the form of the assertion "This is mine; this am I; this is my ego" and makes his reactions the center of an imaginary drama of loss and gain, pleasure and pain, good and bad.

Seeing people everywhere making themselves miserable, the Buddha's teaching was to the point—extinction of suffering, *nirvana*. He rejected, as not to the point, displays of miraculous powers and speculations about metaphysical questions. He urged his followers not to rely on the achievements of others or the understanding of others which might simply be woven into their own dreams: "Be ye a refuge to yourself. Betake yourselves to no external refuge . . . Hold fast to the Truth as a lamp.

Hold fast as a refuge to the Truth. Look not for refuge to anyone besides yourself . . ."[3]

Because of its compassionate urgency, the Buddha's teaching resists comparison with the affirmative teaching of Hinduism. Some have seen in the Buddhist denial of the ego and emphasis on transience a pessimistic rejection of all values. What is negative in Buddhism is not its truth but its way of presenting that truth. The goal is defined negatively—and practically—as release from suffering, ignorance, and selfishness. Confronting a man with the impermanence of the accumulated opinions and sympathies he treasures as himself brings home the ancient warning "not this, not that."

Whatever has been shaped through the law of cause and effect can be reshaped by the same law: "By oneself, indeed is evil done, by oneself is one injured. By oneself is evil left undone, by oneself one is purified."[4] In this spirit, codes of moral behavior serve principally as a preparatory discipline, as a method of purification for the most important task of cultivating "mindfulness." Direct insight into workings of the causal law in oneself is what strikes to the root of all the illusions of the ego and its suffering.

Religion: Three Methods of Realization

PRAYER AND MEDITATION

Prayer might be defined as the method appropriate to belief in a transcendent deity, and meditation as the method appropriate to a religion that aims toward realization of the god within. However, the Hindu prays before his chosen image of the Lord, and the Christian contemplative engages in an activity that is no less properly called meditation than the "sitting" of a Buddhist monk.

In its essence prayer is as little concerned with obtaining favors as the practice of meditation. The experience of a nineteenth-century Hindu provides a vivid example. After several attempts to pray for the relief of his suffering family, he had to give up completely because each time he became aware of the presence of the deity he was so overwhelmed that he found it impossible to ask for anything at all.

In the Islamic tradition, prayer is the fundamental right and responsibility of man by virtue of his central place in the cosmic scheme. By his profession of faith "There is no God but Allah" the Muslim directly affirms the truth of which all creation is an indirect expression. Prayer for the Muslim is both an avowal of faith and a personal act of submission to Allah. The prayers which he recites five times a day include a definite sequence of postures in which the individual stands, bows, and prostrates himself. Thus his body shares in the recognition of his essential dignity as man and his absolute dependence on God.

In the American Indian prayer the individual exposes himself to the powers of the Great Spirit in "crying for a vision." For this, he must have great courage and determination. Guided by a wise man through rituals of purification and dedication, the individual prepares for his vigil, naked and alone on top of a mountain. Only by realizing the depth of his need and the need of the community which shares in any benefit he receives, can the seeker bring himself to pray in the face of his own vulnerability.[5]

In the Judeo-Christian tradition, prayer is the meeting of man and God. According to one figure of Hasidism, the Jewish mystical movement: "The people imagine that they pray before God. But this is not so, for prayer itself is the essence of divinity."[6]

Similarly, a Christian contemplative writing in the fourteenth century compares prayer to the cry for help that burst forth from a man brought to the limits of his resources. The image is meant to suggest wholeness of purpose, not violence: "For now the contemplative must hold himself continually poised and alert at the highest and most sovereign point of his spirit."[7] In this tradition, prayer is an effort to find the place where a man is most himself—the ground of his being—which is, by the mystery of love, the place where he is most related to God.

Each of the religious traditions presents man with the startling claim that he is not really what he takes himself to be. For example, in Christianity, one finds the parable of the king's son who squanders his inheritance to live among swine. Hindu sages declare that the true self is the infinite changeless witness. Buddhism points to belief in a personal identity as the fundamental illusion that produces all suffering.

From the traditional point of view, meditation is the laboratory work in which a man can come to know himself as he is. If meditation has often been dismissed as shallow passivity, it is perhaps because instructions for setting up the laboratory have been mistaken for a description of the experiment itself. A relaxed awareness is regarded as a necessary condition of study, and the influences of the body that contribute to it are carefully taken into account.

The *Bhagavad Gita,* one of the greatest and most widely known texts of Hinduism, recommends a balanced posture for meditation—"with upright body, head, and neck, which rest still and move not; with inner gaze which is not restless . . ."—and the support of a balanced way of life: "Yoga is a harmony. Not for him who eats too much, or for him who eats too little; not for him who sleeps too little, or for him who sleeps too much." Like any scientist making an investigation, the meditator must approach his study impartially—"master of his mind, hoping for nothing, desiring nothing."[8] Working in this way, a seeker may witness in himself the operation of cosmic laws that govern the play of nature—and so disentangle himself from their control. Paradoxically, the method itself demands that one find a way to the "eye of the storm" in order to study its forces.

SCRIPTURE

In the traditions, scripture is sacred, not because it is about religious subjects but because it is a transmission from a higher source of a teaching which man desperately needs. In its essence, as revelation, scripture is regarded as an expression of the same creative intelligence that produced man and the universe.

Jewish mystics studied the Torah, the five books of Moses, in order to discover the laws of divine manifestation. Regarded in its mystical essence as the name of God, the Torah was thought to serve as the instrument of creation. In Christianity it is Christ, the Son, who embodies the truth: "Through Him everything came into being and without Him nothing that exists came into being" (John 1:3).

The link between existence and revelation is found also in the Hindu conception of the Vedas, which, as scripture, record what exceptional men have seen of the unchanging spiritual laws that govern all transformations of matter and energy. But the "eternal Vedas" are these universal laws themselves to which the written record provides a key.

Yet, if there is in scripture a mystery that corresponds to the mystery that is in man, it is not on the surface. According to tradition, scripture responds to a person's preparation and the level at which he experiences his need. When the disciples asked Jesus why he spoke in parables, the answer was a paradox: "For whoever has will receive abundantly, but whoever has not will be deprived of whatever he has" (Matt. 13:12).

As indirect communication, scripture conceals and reveals its truth at the same time. Although its secrets demand preparation, its more accessible levels offer preparation. Commandments and special regulations guide a person in all conditions of life, directing his energies and reminding him of God. According to the great medieval Jewish philosopher Maimonides, even the apparent contradictions found in the Bible are intended to lead the reader to search for a deeper meaning.

In the Koran, which forms the heart and backbone of Islamic faith, the phonetic and symbolic qualities of the Arabic language itself guide the seeker. Like all ancient languages of revelation which are regarded as sacred, Arabic is inherently symbolic. A single word can convey several levels of meaning, from the name of an object to the subtle and elusive meaning of an abstract concept. For this reason, the Koran is considered strictly untranslatable, since any rendering limits the meaning to whatever interpretation corresponds to the translator's level of understanding. To the casual reader, the Koran may show itself as a confusing collection of stories, religious and social regulations, and enticing images of heaven. But the faithful Muslim can read in the early struggles of his religion a symbolic account of an inner war against the forces of dispersal in his own being.

SACRED ART

The idea of sacred art has always been connected with the idea of an exact science of man. Its purpose is to embody a truth in a way that can penetrate superficial associations and opinions and make a deep impression on the inner man.

As an expression of traditional wisdom, the work of art cannot be regarded as the creation of a single craftsman. It was never signed and the artist usually worked within strictly defined rules of measure and proportion. That is not to say that the artist's activity was mechanical. It was the aim of the true craftsman to discover in his work the secrets of all creation. The making of a masterpiece was itself the mark of an initiation into mysteries which could no more be given than skill in a craft.

The art of ancient Egypt, produced by such craftsmen, was designed to convey the cosmic quality of the thing represented. An impersonal causal principle, finding expression in a statue of a god or goddess, could guide a person's emotional awareness past idolatry to an intuitive understanding of that principle's function in himself and the universe.

In the sculptures of black Africa, the proportions of a figure are carefully determined by the artist but apparently without any attempt at a naturalistic representation of the human body. The aim of the traditional African artist was not to make an accurate likeness but to capture a quality so accurately that the figure or carving could attract the corresponding spiritual influence.

A similar conception is found in the miraculous power attributed to the icons or religious paintings of Orthodox Christianity. In the words of a sober twentieth-century writer: "An icon or a cross does not exist simply to direct our imagination during our prayers. It is a material centre in which there reposes an energy, a divine force, which unites itself to human art."[9]

Finally, in the *thanka* art of Tibet, the Westerner may find easier access to a theoretical understanding of sacred art. What in one frame sounds like superstition is here presented in psychological terms. The deities of *thanka* art are represented in the precise posture, expression, and coloring that will show the viewer a particular kind of awareness. In each painting, there is an entire world, a subtle teaching, and a benevolent influence for one who studies it. Yet, in every case, it is nothing other than the viewer himself—his own awareness—that is being discovered and is opening in response.

Religion and the Plight of Modern Man

Having surveyed the teachings and practices of the great world religions, and having attempted to reach some understanding of the general aim of all religious tradition, it remains to examine the place of religious tradition in the contemporary world. As has already been suggested in the introductory section, the present age is witnessing a rebirth of interest in the religious dimension of life—to such an extent that some observers speak of a twentieth-century spiritual renaissance.

On the whole, this spiritual renaissance is taking place outside the structures of the established religious institutions of the West. We shall limit ourselves to discussing two main sources of this current renewal of the religious impulse: the effort to bridge the gap between modern science and ancient spiritual world views, and the eruption, particularly in America, of numerous new religions, most of which find their source in the religions of the Orient.

It is customary to trace the origin of the conflict between religion and Western science back to the theories of Copernicus (1473–1543) and Galileo (1564–1642), concerning the movement of the earth around the sun. As every schoolchild is now taught, the church regarded the Copernican–Galilean picture of the cosmos as a threat to the biblical conception that the earth is the unmoving center of the universe. The generally accepted view is that from then on in the Western world the quest for knowledge of nature was at loggerheads with the demands of faith. Eventually, the explanatory power and pragmatic successes of science overwhelmed the teachings of the church, and the scientific world view prevailed. The ideal of reason triumphed over belief.

Such in simplified form is the popular understanding of the warfare between science and religion. In recent years, however, due in large measure to the influx of Oriental teachings, both the *knowledge* component of religion and the *belief* component of science have come more clearly into view.

In the field of *psychology*, for example, it is now generally recognized that the great mystics of all spiritual traditions understood aspects of human nature which have totally eluded the vision of modern science. Through exposure to Eastern religions, the whole idea of states of consciousness is becoming an increasingly important subject of research among Western psychologists. The issue here is crucial, for it is not simply a matter of studying pathological states of consciousness, such as hallucination, psychosis, and anxiety. The emphasis now is shifting toward the study of *higher* states of consciousness which are characterized not by strange visions, but by increased general intelligence, moral power, and freedom from egoistic emotions. In the light of these studies, a question arises as to the inferior quality of the state of consciousness which characterizes the everyday life of modern man. Such a question is truly revolutionary, for the ability to perceive and explain is itself said to be relative to a man's state. Therefore, the whole scientific conception of reality is put in doubt much more decisively than could ever have been done by opposing literal interpretations of the Bible to the theories of the natural sciences. From this point of view, the crisis of ecology and the dangerously negative social effects of overdeveloped technology are seen to emanate from modern man's failure to understand the states of consciousness that are possible for an individual and which are necessary for right action and impartial understanding, the point being that only in a passionately embraced inferior state of consciousness could mankind have gotten itself into its present dangerous predicament.

The next few years will determine what sort of effect the new interest in spiritual teachings will have on the materialistic world view of Western man. One could list a great many influential psychologists and psychotherapists now studying the mind in the light of traditional teachings as well as eminent physicists turning to Oriental conceptions of cosmic order. In addition, there is a significant movement among medical scientists to understand ancient systems of healing, such as Chinese acupuncture, which are rooted in a spiritual conception of human nature and a nonmaterialistic view of the universe.

Less clearly defined, but perhaps of greatest importance, is the fact that so many Westerners, including many scientists, are now actively practicing methods of *meditation*—some within the Buddhist framework, others within the framework of Hinduism—for example, Transcendental Meditation, which is a radical adaptation of certain aspects of the Hindu Vedanta system.

In the traditional systems, as has been indicated, meditation is one of the chief methods by which the individual can directly experience both the limitedness of his everyday state of consciousness and the possibilities for himself of higher states which bring him into contact with a supreme reality. At the same time, it is through disciplines such as meditation that the individual can witness the purposeful causal forces which operate behind the scenes in the sensory world of everyday life. Modern science gradually separated itself from the idea of a creator God because it had no verifiable evidence for such a being. However, methods such as meditation introduce an entirely new field for empirical observation as well as refining the instrument of observation itself, namely the individual mind. Through practices such as meditation, traditional teachings have offered modern man a means to verify empirically the existence of a supreme intelligence which cannot be seen by the senses, nor proved merely through logical chains of deduction.

The question of critical importance, therefore, is whether modern people who are turning to meditation will do so with the same intent as did traditional man, who was helped in this respect by innumerable aspects of traditional culture, such as certain codes of morality that nourished the spiritual emotions of man. In the ancient traditions, much help was given and much experience was necessary before an individual could profit from the sort of discoveries that can be made in meditative practices. Will modern man make use of these fragments of ancient traditions in the same way, that is, for egoistic purposes, that he has made use of the great discoveries about the external world which were made by modern science? Will he relate to his inner environment with the same attitude that he has related to his outer environment? Upon that issue hinges the crisis of the contemporary religious situation.

The ambiguities of the current religious renaissance are strikingly apparent in the new religions which have taken root in the past decade, particularly in America and England. Numerous helpful catalogues of this phenomenon are available which show that there are literally thousands of groups, small and large, throughout the Western world which have formed around one or another teacher who has migrated from the East. Transcendental Meditation and the so-called "Hare Krishna" movements are only the most well-known examples. Centers for the practical pursuit of Zen Buddhism, directly or indirectly connected to an actual Japanese Zen Master, exist in most major American cities; even lamas from Tibet, such as Chogyam Trungpa, have now gathered large followings which include some of the most sophisticated and influential minds of the present cultural scene. Islamic mysticism (Sufism) has also begun to attract its notable followers, but its success in taking root in the Western world is at present nowhere as marked as that of Buddhism.

Together with this widespread influx of Eastern religions, we are also witnessing a pervasive revival of Pentecostal Christianity which emphasizes the emotional commitment to the person of Christ and which offers its followers a form of intense religious experience that until recently was geographically and sociologically limited in technologically advanced Western societies. The search for Christian methods of meditation and contemplation has also gathered some momentum, particularly under the influence of the writings of the American Trappist monk, Thomas Merton, who was himself strongly influenced by Zen and Tibetan Buddhism.

In all of this, the overriding question is whether traditional modes of spiritual search can be really effective in a world that has almost totally cut its ties to the ancient ways of living. Are the forms by which truth was once transmitted inapplicable to the conditions of modern life? This question insists itself because among the followers of the new religions one often witnesses the process by which only those parts of ancient traditions are accepted which seem relevant or attractive. *Can part of a tradition lead to the same result that once required the complete tradition?* This has always been a problem in the spiritual history of mankind: the tendency of the mind to select out of a teaching only those aspects which it likes, while ignoring other aspects which are also necessary, thereby creating a subjective religion out of a carefully interconnected totality. It is one of the most fundamental meanings of the term "idolatry" in the Judeo-Christian teachings: man must not create his own god. In any event, many of the extraordinary teachers who have come to the West from Asia are wrestling with this question now. Whether they will succeed in transmitting to modern people the workable essence of religion, while adapting the outer aspects to the modern temperament, no one as yet can say.

REFERENCES

1. *The Cloud of Unknowing and the Book of Privy Counseling,* ed. and intro. William Johnston, S.J. (Garden City, New York; Doubleday, Image Books, 1973), p. 150.
2. Shaikh Sharfuddin Maneri or Makhdum-ul-Mulk, *Letters from a Sufi Teacher,* trans. from the Persian by Baijnath Singh (New York: Samuel Weiser, 1974), p. 73.
3. Dīgha-nikāya II, cited in Huston Smith, *The Religions of Man* (New York: Harper and Row, 1958), p. 109.
4. Dhammapada, XII: 9 in *A Sourcebook in Indian Philosophy,* ed. Sarvepelli Radhikrishnan and Charles A. Moore (Princeton: Princeton University Press, 1957), p. 305.

5. See Joseph Epes Brown, *The Sacred Pipe* (Baltimore: Penguin Books, 1972), esp. Ch. IV, *Hanblecheyapi:* Crying for a Vision.
6. Buber, Martin, *Hasidism and Modern Man,* ed. and trans. Maurice Friedman (New York: Harper and Row, 1966), p. 89.
7. *The Cloud of Unknowing and the Book of Privy Counseling,* p. 95.
8. *The Bhagavad Gita,* trans. Juan Mascaro (Baltimore: Penguin Books), Ch. VI: 13, 16, 18.
9. Lossky, Vladimir, *The Mystical Theology of the Eastern Church* (Cambridge and London: James Clarke, 1957), p. 189.

THE USED RELIGIONS

MODERN man, disenchanted by science and by the established forms of his religion, suddenly finds arrayed before him religious teachings emanating out of worlds and times he has never known. From the Orient and the Near East, ancient systems that in the past have been for us little more than food for fantasy now seem to offer themselves as live options, each promising us a renewed and sacred relationship to our own being and to the cosmos that contains us.

One may even detect the apparent stirrings of the ancient contemplative traditions of Christianity and Judaism. Ideas that were once burned into man through the fires of spiritual discipline and an all-encompassing moral code are now, it seems, published and explained by almost everyone, almost everywhere. Not only ideas, however, but spiritual forms and psychophysical disciplines are being brought here by teachers and holy men representing a broad spectrum of alien cultures. Around these teachers from the East gather thousands of people, young and old, drawn by the power of experiences such as were never vouchsafed to them by church or synagogue or by the secular religion of psychiatry.

For anyone who has not been blind and deaf during the past twenty years this development is astounding. One might have expected that political upheavals and advanced technology would produce a superficially internationalized world in the area of economics, or in the arts, or on the external levels of religious fashions. But knowing that the great religious founders of the past deeply embedded their teachings in the milieu of a specific culture with all its special needs and psychic traits, and recognizing that the passage of a genuine teaching from one culture to another is an event nearly as extraordinary and rare as the original appearance of the teaching itself, one may well be skeptical. Two of the great missionary teachings of the world, Christianity and Buddhism, transformed the life of entire peoples—but over long periods of time and, particularly in Buddhism, working quietly and from within. In Tibet and China, for example, centuries passed before the impulse given by Padmasambhava or Bodhidharma was reflected in the general culture. And who knows what took place between the time when the first Christians migrated to Britain and the time when the forms of Celtic Christianity touched the existence of all people living there? How many hundreds of years passed while the deserts of the Near East sheltered the early cenobites? Is so much time and silence needed for the gathering of a certain energy?

I am writing as a Californian, a man without tradition who hears all around him claims of a spiritual revolution being made not only by the representatives of alien traditions but by countless people like himself who have hardly ever felt the breath of traditional spirituality in their lives. Without much real concern for the historical background, many of these thousands see the present moment as the beginning of a new age: They are confident the future will be different from the past.

But other voices tell us that, far from being a sign of an awakening, this phenomenon of the new religions is only the most recent turn in modern man's descent into total materialism: the movement from anti-traditionalism to an even more sinister countertraditionalism in which the truth of ancient teachings is parodied through the same forces of exploitation that have defined the entire modern era.

What will help us find our way out of this ambiguity? I ask the question as a Californian. Is it true that the ancient spiritual teachings are now coming forward and offering themselves as living alternatives to Western man? Is it in America, in California—where scarcely a trace remains of traditional civilization—that this astonishing transaction will be made? Or is it too late for everything except imitation, enthusiastic commitment, and the other devices by which confusion is masked?

Out of these questions yet another question arises, perhaps even more fundamental: *Are the forms by which truth was once transmitted inapplicable to the present conditions of human life?* Can we discover with precision the specific point of failure in the relationship between ourselves and the sacred? For, *without knowing how to find this point of failure, how will we situate ourselves at the correct point of effort?* And if we cannot so situate ourselves, will not everything that is presented to us as spiritual struggle be largely a waste of time, or even worse?

Our question is twofold: who has failed—ourselves or the traditions? What is the real hiddenness and the real corruption of tradition?

It was with such questions in mind that I recently traveled through Europe, and I offer the following recollection in the hope of opening these issues further. For what it meant to be an American, a modern man, a Californian, finally began to be clear to me at the end of my tour, among the monasteries of Mount Athos.

I had often dreamed of visiting this place, the monastic heart of the Eastern Church. Cut off from the world for a thousand years, was it a Western Tibet where there still existed the knowledge and methods of esoteric Christianity? By that, I mean the knowledge of man's true weaknesses and hidden possibilities, as well as the techniques of inner prayer, bodily discipline, and communal relationship that could destroy the weaknesses and bring forth the possibilities. I was convinced that such knowledge was not the special preserve of the Oriental traditions. Yet I had never found anything in the existing forms of Western Christianity to support my conviction. My purpose was to discover if these ancient spiritual practices of Western Christianity were coming to life again. Yet my search had so far discovered only one tantalizing hint outside the shadows of the Vatican—a word spoken by a magnetic woman, a devout Christian mystic, who said only that the church had kept its secrets too well. What secrets? She did not wish to say more.

And so it was with intense anticipation that I was carried along the rugged Aegean coast toward the peninsula of Athos on the last leg of my journey. I tried to maintain a realistic sense of restraint, for I had been warned from all sides that the cenobitic tradition was dying here and that many of the monasteries were now abandoned relics tended only by a few die-hard monks. The population, I was told, had sunk from twenty thousand monks to a low of fifteen hundred and was still declining.

I will not go into great detail about the appearance of the island and its ancient monasteries, the dense vegetation, the stench of compost filling the air, the disarray and windy desolation of the official buildings, and, for me, the pervasive impression of something disturbingly familiar: the bearded, patriarchal monks in their black robes going mechanically about their business in ways that resembled the orthodox Jews I knew in my childhood. I traced this sense of familiarity to the feeling I always had as a child when forced to participate in the austere forms of a tradition that was meaningless to me and that had no right in my world.

From the very first step on Athos the question rang in my mind: what *is* tradition? Is there a life I cannot see within these forms? Is it because I lack real spiritual hunger? But if that is so, what do I—what do we—hunger for when we ask over and over again about the meaning of our existence and when we feel the contradictions—which no science or philosophy has resolved—between the narrowness of our lives and the vast universal forces of death, creation, and cosmic harmony? If a spiritual tradition cannot meet us on the ground of this hunger for meaning, then with whom does the failure lie?

Before taking to the trails, I sat for a while in the Cathedral of Karyes, the central village of the peninsula. In the Gothic cathedrals of Western Europe one is instantly shocked into silence by their immeasurable vertical spaces, until gradually the extraordinary light breaking in through the stained-glass windows gently lifts one upward. The universe of the Gothic cathedral is to me immense and merciful. But the Orthodox church is dark as a starry night, lit mainly by scattered flickering candles. In this space one is everywhere closely surrounded by the powerful icons, radiating as though by their own light. One's eyes move over walls covered with stars against a night-blue background, stopping suddenly at the great dome above, upon which a gigantic head of Christ looks back down at you. This is a cosmos whose central force is an act of sacrifice for the sake of man, for oneself. And this sacrificial cosmos demands from man a response. But by the time I left Athos I was wondering from where in us this response could possibly come.

After several hours of hiking I came to the fortress-like Stavroniketa monastery jutting out dramatically over the sea on the eastern coast of the peninsula. By custom, each monastery is obliged to take in all sojourners and provide them with food and lodging. But I was turned away at Stavroniketa: because of repairs there was no room for guests.

No amount of persuasion on my part (in an exchange of clumsy gestures and broken English) had any effect. I was tremendously disappointed, having heard that at this monastery something might be found. And of course I knew that, had they really wished, they could surely have taken in a single guest for the night. It was late in the afternoon and, knowing the monasteries close their doors at sundown, I wearily stood outside the Stavroniketa pondering my next move. Huge storm clouds were gathering overhead, leaving me with the prospect of a dash of several kilometers down the coast.

What was I looking for? I realized, standing there, that I was traveling blind. Did I expect to encounter some aged hermit with piercing eyes who would take me in and reveal to me the secrets of his practice? Or would the abbot of some great monastery allow me to participate in the rituals of his inner circle? Moreover, I spoke no Greek, so that in addition to everything else I was naïvely hoping for a miracle of language as well.

How far I was from California! Not once during all my earlier investigations of the new religious groups of America did I ever feel something was being held back from me. Whether it was a Zen monastery or a Sufi group or a fledgling ashram, always the leaders invited me in. Even when told it was an esoteric teaching, I had little difficulty arranging to participate as much as I wished; and even when warned that there were things that could not be spoken about to outsiders, I found that sooner or later more information was given to me than I had asked for. All that had surprised me at first, but I soon came to take it for granted. Now, however, and in the next twenty-four hours, I was again faced with the question as to the nature of spiritual reserve and the maturity of California religion.

I was about to give up and move on when, as though out of nowhere, there appeared a layman who addressed me in perfect English. I told him what I was and what I was looking for, and, to make the story brief, in two hours I found myself high in the turret of the monastery in a spacious, austere guest room. Seated across from me was Father Vasileios, abbot of Stavroniketa. This was the setting of the long conversation that then took place between Father Vasileios and me. I believe that in this conversation it may be possible to find the essential questions we in the modern world need to place before all of the traditional teachings that are offering themselves to us.

The sky had cleared, and through the wide-open windows the room was lit by the twilight and the rising moon reflected off the sea. We sat around a heavy plank table—Father Vasileios in his black robes and hat, and our interpreter, a young professor of medicine from Athens who wished to be known only by the name Evangelos.

As for Father Vasileios, he did not seem very much older than I—in his mid-forties, perhaps, slender and athletic with aquiline features, a full, black beard, and noncommittal, steady eyes. I began by describing to him the profusion of new religious groups in America, the influx of teachers from the East, and the massive movement away from established religious forms by the young. I chose to emphasize the fact that most of these new religions bring with them practical methods such as meditation, chanting, Yoga exercises, and the like which seem to provide real experiences of something Christianity and Judaism have only been talking about. I had in the back of my mind an interesting comment made to me only a week before by an official at the Vatican. He had said that for too long there had been fear of spiritual experiences—as though people had ceased to believe that God is good enough to give such experiences.

"It is not a question of methods," said Father Vasileios. "It is a question of the whole of life. These methods produce hallucinations. What do I mean by hallucinations? People search after experiences, not truth.

One must begin by accepting truth and feeling truth. Only then can 'method' enter in the right way."

I found this reply very interesting. There was something *contemporary* in it, which I suppose I should have anticipated from a few facts I had gleaned from Evangelos about the abbot's background. He had studied for several years in Paris (our conversation took place in a mixture of French, Greek, and English) and he was, I gathered, the only abbot on Athos who had been involved even to that extent in modern Western culture.

"But," I said, "our religions in the West long ago reached the point where they seemed incapable of providing new experiences. The young—and the older generation—finally have reacted to this lack. Is it so wrong to look for special experiences? When life loses its meaning— then what else should a man struggle for if not for a new contact with reality? a new quality of experience?"

After a slight pause, he answered with one word, "Faith."

He waited while I tried to digest that. I felt a wave of disappointment. Yes, I understood his answer; it was good Christian doctrine; in a way it was the great truth. But in another way, the great truth was not enough and could not be enough for us. We needed more than pure truth; we needed help. For twentieth-century man, was there enough psychological help in the answer "faith"?

From Father Vasileios I felt an immediate awareness of my disappointment. I have interviewed many religious leaders before and since meeting Father Vasileios. With very many of them—the representatives of the new religions no less than church officials—I have felt that their replies to my questions were preformulated. But it seemed to me that some were searching for their own truth at the very moment of their replying to me, reconstituting their understanding, as it were, out of the unknown. The ring of authority, which is a much more mysterious factor than we imagine, existed for me only in the latter cases. Father Vasileios seemed constantly to be shifting between these two places.

Of course, the quality of my questioning was probably not such as to deserve more than doctrinaire answers. I think we must bear that factor in mind when we try to put questions to the great traditions. We so easily assume that our questions deserve great answers.

"One must *begin* with faith," he said, "and from that God adds what is necessary. Anything else is human invention."

"In America," I said, "many young people begin with the prayer of Jesus."

I expected him to raise his eyebrows at this because I knew that in the

Orthodox tradition it is considered dangerous to practice the prayer of Jesus, the repetition of the phrase "Lord Jesus Christ have mercy on me," without the guidance of a spiritual director. I felt I was still not getting across to him what psychological method means to us in America. In fact, throughout my travels in Europe I was amazed at how traditional religious leaders—men who had the reputation of being spiritual leaders and even mystics—were satisfied with words, thoughts, concepts. I thought at first that surely these leaders were quite justifiably concealing from me, a mere outsider, the hidden practical side of their discipline. As I have already mentioned, the whole idea of spiritual reserve or secrecy was taking on a new importance to me. Yet now, sitting across from Father Vasileios, I had for a moment the same unpleasant feeling I experienced throughout my trip—that the only secrets left in Christianity were yet more words and thoughts.

Father Vasileios was not at all surprised. He was quite aware that Westerners were learning about Orthodoxy through two or three books that centered around the prayer of Jesus. I saw him searching for a way to reply to an American's—or a nonbeliever's—lack of comprehension. Finally, he answered me at great length on the subject of grace and its relationship to emotion. He spoke of the Jesus prayer as a form of worship and said that all worship requires sincerity and humility. Purity of feeling could not come through anything but the acceptance of the blood of Christ.

I cannot here convey the intensity with which he spoke—I mean to say the quality of attention that he compelled from me by the evenness of his thought.

I felt warmed by the tremendous effort he was obviously making to communicate to me. I began to grasp the teachings of Orthodox Christianity in a way that had never before been possible for me. In the long silences I watched the darkness settling in the room and enjoyed the balmy night wind that began to blow off the sea. But during these silences there were several moments when I glancingly observed something important take place in myself: I saw the believer in myself begin to arise and step forward.

Let me say at once that concerning the *faith* of which Jesus Christ spoke I know nothing, and it is not this of which I am now speaking. What I saw in myself I have seen many times before and I have seen it in others—indeed I have sometimes succeeded, not to my credit, in provoking it in others. If I call it belief, or the believer, I do not mean to limit it only to the religious sphere, though surely it is in that sphere that it is the most insidious in its action.

I do not think it is necessary here to attempt a psychological description of this process. Suffice it to say that this belief has the taste of inner violence about it. It is connected with certain kinds of emotional stress and the wish to resolve this stress, combined with a tiny, ephemeral element of intellectual grasp, with personal attractions, with fears of various sorts, and all presenting itself under the banner of "the imperative to choose"—commitment—as though any sort of real freedom of choice is possible in this fog of self-deception and hidden fragmentation.

How much of what we often call religious passion on the battleground of the freedom of the will is really only this state of confusion? What is the real struggle for faith? Don't we flatter ourselves thinking that we are on a level of consciousness in which this struggle is even possible? We very much need to ponder this question, which touches upon one of the most significant ways we have distorted the idea of mercy and catholicity in Christianity, thereby avoiding the recognition that we need help in order to be brought to the ability to choose.

So with Father Vasileios I continued to press the topic of method—searching for another way of putting it so as to get away from the suggestion of a mere technique or manipulative device.

"In all the great traditions," I said, "there seems to be a common idea of mercy or compassion that goes hand in hand with the idea of justice and rigor. But isn't it more than an idea? Aren't there practical expressions of this mercy—and, if so, aren't they based on a precise knowledge of the human organism—the emotional strengths and weaknesses, the influence of the body on the psyche and vice versa?

"To me, it is obvious," I continued, "that many contemporary people feel in Yoga or Zen something that comes closer to mercy in action, even though the word mercy is hardly ever used in comparison with Christianity.

"What I mean is that they feel—to some extent—that the workings of their minds and bodies are being understood. Therefore they sense communication being offered. To be helped to sit quietly, to begin to observe directly the transitoriness and gradations of the thoughts that govern our lives: isn't such a thing necessary before or at least at the same time that one exhorts someone to faith?"

I was about to go on in this vein, sweeping aside all my reservations about the way Americans naïvely gobbled up Orientalisms of various sorts. I risked exaggerating the success of Eastern religion in America because I was now sure that Father Vasileios did not fully grasp the need that was being felt in America—in California—for a new quality of psychological experience.

But he interrupted me with a quiet laugh, and startled both me and my interpreter. "I could tell you of things a thousand times better than your Yoga," he said.

Evangelos's eyes opened wide as he momentarily dropped his role of interpreter. He turned his whole body toward Father Vasileios, and my ignorance of Greek did not prevent me from understanding what Evangelos was asking. Father Vasileios answered him a little curtly and then, speaking in French, went on to another topic as though regretting that he had let something slip.

"What did he say?" I asked.

"I asked him what things he was speaking about," said Evangelos, in a state of barely concealed excitement and disappointment. "He answered that he only meant the Jesus prayer and such things. . . ."

The conversation moved on. It was getting quite late; the moon was high and no longer visible through the windows. In the darkness we could barely make out each other's faces.

"Do you believe that tradition ever changes?" I asked. "By tradition, I mean the rituals, the liturgy, the forms. Are not adaptations necessary in the light of changing circumstances, changes in people's problems and habits of living and thinking?"

"The liturgy," said Father Vasileios, "embraces the whole of life from birth . . . or before birth . . . until death. How could it change? It is permanent. Yet, at the same time, it is in constant movement. . . . Within the liturgy a man must find the liturgy within himself. We must become a new being. Every minute a man converts, every instant he becomes Orthodox . . ."

More and more, as he spoke, my admiration grew for this man's refusal to stand outside Orthodoxy in order to explain it to me. Yet at the same time I began to feel an impulse to bring the conversation down to earth. And so I presumed to interrupt him again. "What about other religions?"

Evangelos phrased my blunt question in such a way that Father Vasileios thought I was asking about ecumenicism.

He took a long time before replying. "The Church must confess, not discuss. Orthodoxy is like Jesus in the world. It has the truth for anyone who wants it. Like Jesus, it says 'I am.' It can do no more. Like Jesus, it says 'Not my will, but Thy will.' "

Father Vasileios leaned forward toward me in the darkness. I could just make out his eyes and the rest of his features. What he then said to me contained such poignancy that it brought all my questioning to an end.

"The Church knows that other teachings are attracting the young. It knows that if it changed certain things, that would not be happening. But it must remain what it is. It does so with tears. It knows that it drives people away."

I waited, and then turned to Evangelos to signal that for my part I had nothing more to ask. But no one moved.

I returned to California with more questions than answers. I had begun my journey wondering what modern man must do to *hear* the teachings of tradition as they were intended to be heard—with that in us which is able to hear them. But just here a great difficulty presents itself. Are the present conditions in which we live such that it is possible to hear these teachings? For it is surely an error to believe that merely by listening to words and experiencing a conversion of feeling we will be able to take in the teachings of the masters in a way that touches the whole of our being. Must not a spiritual teaching reach even further down to us—and *help us to hear*?

Are the teachings a means or an end? A means of listening or an end to be listened to? Of what lasting value would it be were I to accept the truth and yet remain ignorant of my inherent tendency to distort the truth? Must there not be a way of presenting sacred ideas which at the same time awakens in man the faculty of listening? Without this little awakening—as we may call it—it seems naïve to hope for the great awakening. Without it, I shall unconsciously accept or reject great ideas with the same partiality or violence that I accept or reject all the other ideas, divine or demonic, that the world presents to me. I shall become a believer or a doubter—and the history of civilization is witness to the fact that even great ideas become a destructive influence when they are used to mask ignorance of ourselves.

It is this little awakening—without which nothing is possible—that I believe has been forgotten in Western religion, and this forgetting has generated much of the confusion and mischief of dogmatic religion and modern psychology.

For, consider: I had to travel nearly halfway around the world, and only then, with extraordinary luck, was I able to speak to an exceptional man *under conditions that were the manifestation of an idea.* I offer this as speculation, as my own impression. I cannot speak from certainty. But the long voyage, the anticipation, the physical and financial difficulties, the ambience of Athos—its beauty and repulsiveness (again I am speaking subjectively)—all of this and much else: my particular fatigue, my *need* to understand something, the darkening room, the straining to understand the language, the attempt to read the eyes of Vasileios—I could go on with this guesswork. My point is that I came to understand a fragment of Orthodox Christianity only under conditions that to some extent reflected a true idea about man (myself) as he is and man as he can become, conditions corresponding to the double nature of man, a being partly divine (in his wish for truth) and partly animal (in his egoistic understanding of it). In any case, in these conditions, I *listened*. I will not even say that I was *able* to listen, only that to some extent listening was able to take place.

I do not know to what extent these conditions were intentional or accidental. I believe it was the latter, but this issue is not central to my question. I am simply saying that I have met many men, some of whom were possibly men of even greater spiritual intelligence and of even greater articulateness than this good Father Vasileios. But, apart from a few very notable exceptions, real listening was never able to take place. All the talk in the world about spiritual methods can no longer obscure, for me, the fact that genuine spiritual method begins with the conditions under which ideas are given and under which they are received.

What little I know of the life of ancient man makes me suspect that under the conditions of life that once existed (and that perhaps still exist in parts of Asia) man was more exposed to both sides of his nature. We may surmise that the external conditions of traditional society contained factors to remind men of what they lose through their egoism—so that even in the midst of man's perversity and brutality, as well as in the midst of his apparent moments of triumph, he was not without the help of a cosmic, universal scale by which to taste directly his insignificance and dependence. Modern writers who hold up their violence or injustice of the past as marks of its inferiority fail to consider that a higher civilization is not necessarily one in which men behave like angels, but in which men can experience *both* their divinity and their animality.

If we understand divine love to be the manifestation of truth on the plane of earth, then surely what we are speaking about here is the establishment of conditions—psychological and physical—that are the manifestation of the truth about man. Nowadays, everyone will agree that verbal and intellectual formulations are only one, and perhaps not the most essential, expression of truth. For example, we see in the symbolism of sacred art the transmission of ideas directly into the emotions of man, into that heart that can speak in active voice to the intellect that chooses and is able to attend, to listen to it. Yet perhaps more essential—or, for us, more basic, more necessary—even than art or verbal formulations is the establishment of conditions of living that reflect truth, the truth about ourselves—conditions that make listening possible. Thus the mercy or compassion of a teaching consists not only in the contents it brings but in the conditions under which it brings them. To separate the contents of a teaching from the conditions in which it can be heard can result only in arid scholasticism or blind fanaticism.

In order not to be misunderstood, I wish to make clear something about the meaning of the word "conditions" that is implicit in everything that I have been saying. By stressing the conditions that are necessary for the reception of truth, I do not mean to endorse certain external arrangements, such as robes or communes or rules of conduct, while condemning others. In general, that is how we always tend to look at these things and it has really led us nowhere. We tend to think that external conditions by themselves can be good or bad, useful or harmful.

But that is only dogma in the form not of words but of physical arrangements. Dogmatic ideas are found not only in books but also in the structuring of surroundings, behavior, and rules.

We forget our real inner situation when we think in this way. For we ourselves are such deeply conditioned beings, so passive and suggestible, that no external conditions, however inspired, can by themselves lead us to anything more than new forms of blind dependence. Even inner conditions, such as breathing techniques or special postures of meditation, are not always helpful.

Yet help is necessary. So there is the mystery: how to find that particular angle of vision or inner attitude in which one looks at all things from the perspective of a search for one's own understanding. Merely adding or subtracting outer forms will not automatically produce this attitude.

Here we are in front of a little-noted problem about the struggle for consciousness: external help is possible only to someone who can face the conditions offered from the point of view of a learner. In order to reflect the truth about man, given conditions must contain the demand that we search for this attitude toward ourselves at the very moment of submission to them.

Herein, surely, lies one of the roots of the confusion we suffer from in California and perhaps in the modern world. By themselves, great works of art or true ideas cannot effect real change in man. The energy one receives from ideas or experiences cannot be contained by "fallen" man and serves only further to activate the very weaknesses that made him require these ideas in the first place. Witness the destruction brought about by modern science's hasty application of ideas that in the milieu of past civilizations were reserved for the initiate, or in any case given in a form and under conditions in which men could take them in alongside impressions of their own helplessness and dependence. (I am referring to such ideas as those of the infinite universe and of the idea of human evolution.)* Thus, though the sacred impulse to learn for oneself was the germ of modern science, it rapidly became a destructive influence because of the conditions of living that prevailed in the modern era, conditions that corresponded to no great truth about man but that only manifested man's excessive desire for comfort and egoistic security.

It has been said that the greatness of Western man lies in his impulse to *act* in accordance with truth, an impulse that receives its supreme expression in the teachings of the Old Testament. We know that in modern times this impulse to act was for one reason or another cut off from the sense of a higher truth. The result has been a haste to promote and apply great ideas not fully digested or understood—again, the disastrous results of scientific technology and various political ideologies are witness to this. Our sorrow is that we do not act from ideas but from our reaction to ideas, reactions that are part of what the Eastern traditions call the "desire-nature" and what Western religion once spoke of as the "carnal body," the flesh. I think this is a basic fact about our present situation and accounts for many of our difficulties. Therefore, if sacred ideas are to be transmitted to us, it must be under conditions that take this fact about our nature into full account. But where shall we find the truth transmitted under conditions that enable us simultaneously to study this fact about ourselves and to witness it in action and therefore to see directly the process by which great ideas are distorted in ourselves and made into their opposite, even while the verbal formulations remain intact? The mere preservation of conceptual formulations, rituals, and sacred texts cannot help if the conditions under which these are given us do not open us at the same time to a direct experience of our distortion process.

The study of the movement between psychological states is therefore a necessity for us. The state of wonder, the sense of the sacred, even the collectedness of the state of meditative silence pass over into ordinary inattention and violence, self-deception and sentimentality, breeding cruelty or resentment or subhuman softness. Where shall we find help to study the process that takes place when, for example, I walk from within the sacred space of a Gothic cathedral (or from the state engendered in me by systems of ideas that are like cathedrals) into the pulls and shocks of twentieth-century life? Is there a teaching that so intimately understands the processes of twentieth-century life that it can create condi-

---

* This point is developed more fully in my book *A Sense of the Cosmos: The Encounter of Modern Science and Ancient Truth* (New York: E. P. Dutton, 1977).

tions in which this movement, this pull outward and downward from truth into the hypnosis of our era, can be witnessed, studied, and accepted in full? *That,* I suggest, would be compassion.

There are many modern observers of the present American religious scene who praise the increasing hunger for experience. But do we in America really see what we want from experience? External action seems to have reached its limits in the world around us—the promises of pragmatism are foundering against the crises of environmental destruction, meaningless pleasures, and increased social despair. Is our search for inner experience only the application of the lust for action to the inner life? Are our emotions and thoughts like forests and rivers that we manipulate with the same disastrous love of progress that has brought us to the edge of physical extinction?

In short, not even great spiritual methods brought from authentic sources and preserved intact throughout time can of themselves help us. Nor can great ideas or sacred art. Not just new experiences but wider experiences of ourselves are what we need so that the energy produced by spiritual techniques or great ideas is not squandered in the old ways. And as for these wider experiences of ourselves, of our whole nature as double beings in twentieth-century life, where shall we find the conditions to attract us to such experiences?

I remind you that I speak as a Californian. Yet I suspect that what has been called "Californialand"—a state of confusion mixed with the raw hunger for transcendence—exists throughout the Americanized world. As an inhabitant of "Californialand" I ask of what use would it be were we suddenly to surround ourselves with sacred symbols once again, or even with ancient patterns of community relationship? Without some help that would enable us to touch those deeper layers of feeling in ourselves that can open our eyes to our egoism, which accepts, believes, trusts, and distorts everything, how could traditional patterns of life transform our being?

We are surrounded by countless new religions. At the same time, teachers from the Orient and the Middle East are struggling to preserve and transmit their own traditions within the frame of Western society, where the political conditions, the affluence, and the emotional needs conspire to offer tolerance to any teaching that brings striking ideas about man or new inner experiences.

But can a teaching, however authoritative, be true for us if it persuades us to exercise a faculty that we do not possess, a faculty that is itself the product of long spiritual work? How many of these new religions urge us to accept one set of ideas, to enter into a particular stream

of practice, while rejecting others? What is the meaning of the call for
choice to men who have no power of real choice?

What is needed, I conclude, is a teaching in which *we are known,* not
only for what we can become but for what we are—a teaching that provides us with both experiences of our possibilities and impressions of our
actuality, our real egoism, and our possible freedom. Surely the power to
choose can be born only when we stand in the center, between these two
qualities of experience. And, I feel sure, without our being situated between these two experiences no ideas from whatever sacred source can
act as a guide in the struggle for consciousness of self.

I think the central reason modern psychology undermined the established religions of the West was that through psychology we realized
that we had not been known. The ideas of Christianity and Judaism
were suddenly revealed to be, for us, mere ideals. With the psychologists
we finally felt known.

But, as time has shown, not deeply known. Therein lies the disillusionment with modern psychology. The scale was too small against
which we measured our failures as human beings. So that all the self-
acceptance in the world (which was the mercy of modern psychology)
could not help us, but kept us mired in illusions about ourselves. In attempting to free us from neurotic guilt, psychology only helped us for a
time to feel comfortable about ourselves but never to discover the struggle for greater being. The reason for the method of self-acceptance was
too small, too egoistic and introverted.

Yet, although it fails by exaggerating the importance of its partial insights about the human personality, modern psychology leaves us with
the hope for ideas and methods that can actually work real changes in
ourselves. No wonder teachings have now appeared that attempt to
connect sacred traditions with the general orientation of modern psychology!

The truth is, we lack the touchstone by which to recognize an authentic path of self-knowledge. The real hiddenness and the real corruption
of tradition stems from the ignorance of this fact.

But does this mean we ought to abandon the question of how to recognize what knowledge we need? Quite the contrary. It *is* our question,
and to deny it is to deny our starting point.

But there is another question, equally fundamental, that must be
asked at the same time but that we rarely ask in a serious way. That
question is, "What does it mean to learn?"

The first question—that of recognizing authenticity—when taken
alone, drives us outward in the effort to experience external reality by

our own lights (and is thus the origin of modern science). This movement outward is something dogmatic religion obstructs, even though it wishes to do good by shaping our thought to conform to great ideas. Perhaps there is a place for dogmatic religion in a culture that still allows for the shocks of real experiences—death, physical effort, and the intensity of harmonious sexual experience. But as cultures and nations now interact with an increasingly accidental and violent quality, the experiences available in any modern community tend to become both more uniform and more excessive—overwhelming shocks interspersing the general drift toward ease and self-deception.

In the absence of the necessary real experiences, religious dogma or ill-digested experiences edge man into the wastelands of mental or emotional identity, the closure of thought or feeling around great ideas or experiences that are never understood by the whole person in body and heart.

But the question "What does it mean to learn?" has the power to lead us inward to observe for ourselves what is required if the parts of our inner nature are to come together if only for an instant. A man who realizes that he has never observed this inner process and therefore does not understand or accept the conditions of real learning is in a better position to question the criteria he sets up for a teacher or a teaching. Without asking this question, without realizing that we do not know what great learning demands of us, we abandon ourselves merely to finding a teaching with credentials.

We need to acknowledge that there are two kinds of learning—one given, as is said, by life and the other by books. Even the previous generation maintained this distinction, which has played an important role in American life and has been one of the factors that distinguished American life, for all its faults, from that of the more sophisticated European civilization. But the present generation in this country has obliterated even that weakened version of the distinction between what a man learns with the whole of himself and what he learns only with his mind—that is to say, what he takes in as material for the growth of a new consciousness and what he takes in for utilitarian reasons of comfort, psychological safety, or physical pleasure.

The new generation of Americans who have been captured by drugs, encounter groups, Eastern religion, or the Jesus movement have this one thing in common with the generation that precedes them: all were raised and educated by a system that tried to consider both emotional and mental factors as part of ordinary learning. Up until rather recent times, modern civilization, for all its antitraditionalism, left the development of the emotional life to the family. The mother's role in this was of overwhelming importance. A person had to find himself somewhere in between his mother and the shocks of life. The place of the father was as a representative of aspiration. Mother and father therefore had the task of preparing a person to grow in the midst of life and not to forget God. In this respect, regarding the subtle uniqueness of feeling that arises in the child and that can be maintained through adolescence only with the support of a family reality containing in some measure the aspiration of man, the family was always the first spiritual teacher, or in any event the preparer of the psyche for the spiritual teacher.

The spread of public education and the growth of psychoanalysis and other psychological theories resulted in the mixing of book learning with emotional training sometimes explicitly carried out by educational theorists and often carried out by schoolteachers who themselves believed in the theories of the psychologists.

Public emotional training placed the emphasis on connecting feelings and performance, assuming that feelings were for the support of the ego rather than a special and irreplaceable access to a higher intelligence. The uniqueness of feeling was drowned out by the noise of general emotional training. As a result, the most essential element of real learning was completely forgotten in modern culture: namely, that man can learn from life only to the extent that he can accept the suffering such learning demands.

What sort of suffering? This is a difficult question that cannot be answered merely from theory. I believe that almost everyone, if he tries, can remember in his life an occasion when he turned away from the process of deep learning. Perhaps it was in the moment of a grievous shock such as the death of a loved one, or when abruptly awakening to oneself in the midst of awesome nature or overwhelming physical pain, or when dealt the sort of sudden personal disappointment that pulls out from under one's feet all the illusions about life that support our sense of direction.

In those moments, for a fleeting second, a voice can sometimes be heard within us that comes from a world we never knew existed. In those moments we see that there are actually two levels of reality within our nature. We sometimes describe this experience by saying that everything seemed unreal. But that is not exact. Closer to the truth is that for an instant I realize that this voice is always speaking and that it is I who continually turn away from it. In those exceedingly rare moments, when I am present to the two consciousnesses within my nature, I see that it is not the world that is unreal—it is myself who am a lie. And then, so swiftly that I do not even notice, I am willingly absorbed by all the smaller voices—all the forces of ordinary life—and I "come back to myself."

It would be quite wrong to think of such moments as peak experiences or mystical visions. They are nothing of the kind. But surely, without them, without accepting what they teach us about ourselves, and without the help we require in order to find our way to them more often, not even great ideas or ancient spiritual techniques can change our lives. For, without this acceptance of our blindness to the two natures within us, the living knowledge of the great traditions will fall upon a consciousness that eternally crucifies the truth upon the cross of our unseen egoism.

Into the present milieu many traditional teachers bring ideas, doctrines, and methods of the past, speaking to men and women who do not know what it means to learn and who, because of the disintegration of the family, do not have access to subtle feeling and who therefore trust only the egoistic emotions which are the by-product of the hopeless struggle for mental or emotional identity. Teachers who come to America from more traditional surroundings seem unaware of how far this process has gone here in the West and are perhaps deceived by the apparent willingness of thousands to listen to them.

As I see it, therefore, it is not the content of our beliefs that makes us an antitraditional society, or even the forms of our behavior. It is rather the ease with which we ignore the distinction between two kinds of learning—so much so that the deeper learning, the reception of real experiences for the sake of forging inward connections between the vast scales of reality that exist in man, is forgotten. And with it is forgotten the possible evolution of man as a being between two worlds.

PSYCHIATRY AND THE SACRED

MODERN psychiatry arose out of the vision that man must change himself and not depend for help upon an imaginary God. Over half a century ago, mainly through the insights of Freud and through the energies of those he influenced, the human psyche was wrested from the faltering hands of organized religion and was situated in the world of nature as a subject for scientific study. The cultural shock waves were enormous and long-lasting. But equal to them was the sense of hope that gradually took root throughout the Western world. To everyone, including those who offered countertheories to psychoanalysis, the main vision seemed indomitable: science, which had brought undreamt-of power over external nature, could now turn to explaining and controlling the inner world of man.

The era of psychology was born. By the end of the Second World War many of the best minds of the new generation were magnetized by a belief in this new science of the psyche. Under the conviction that a way was now open to assuage the confusion and suffering of humanity, the study of the mind became a standard course of work in American universities. The ranks of psychiatry swelled, and its message was carried to the public through the changing forms of literature, art, and educational theory. Against this juggernaut of new hope, organized religion was helpless. The concepts of human nature which had guided the Judeo-Christian tradition for two thousand years had now to be altered and corrected just as three hundred years earlier the Christian scheme of the cosmos retreated against the onslaught of the scientific revolution.

But although psychiatry in its many forms pervades our present culture, the hope it once contained has slowly ebbed away. The once charismatic psychoanalyst has become encapsulated within the workaday medical establishment, itself the object of growing public cynicism. The behaviorist who once stunned the world by defining man as a bundle of manageable reactions finds himself reduced to mere philosophizing and to the practice of piecemeal psychological cosmetics. In the burgeoning field of psychophysiology the cries of "breakthrough" echo without real conviction before the awesome and mysterious structure of the human brain. And as for experimental psychology, it has become mute; masses of data accumulated over decades of research with animals remain unrelated and seemingly unrelatable to the suffering, fear, and frustration of everyday human life.

The growing feeling of helplessness among psychiatrists and the cries for help from the masses of modern people operate in perverse contrast to the constant psychologizing of the media. Amid the "answers" provided by publications ranging in sophistication from *Reader's Digest* to *Psychology Today,* millions seem quite simply to have accepted that their lives have no great direction and ask only for help to get them through the night. The once magical promise of a transformation of the mind through psychiatry has quietly disappeared.

Of course, questions about the meaning of life and death and one's relationship to the universe may still tear at a person's insides. But now neither psychiatry nor the church is able to respond even from the same gut level at which such questions can arise—far less from a level of universal knowledge and intuitive relationship which perceives certain cries for help as the seed of the desire for self-transformation.

No one suffers from this lack more than the psychiatrists themselves, more and more of whom despair over their inability to help other human beings in the fundamental way they once dreamed possible. Faced with the accelerating pressure of technology upon the normal patterns of human life, faced with the widespread effects of modern man's twisted relationship to nature, and yearning for a coherent purpose in living, they have come to see themselves as being in the same situation as their patients and the rest of us.

Such, in brief, is the background of a new question that is now arising concerning the hidden structure and distortions of man's inner life. Over the past decade there has taken place in our culture a widespread attraction to ideas and spiritual methods rooted in the ancient traditions of Asia and the Near East. Starting in California, this movement initially had all the earmarks of a fad, a youthful reaction against the excesses of scientism and technocracy. This spiritual revolution still retains many characteristics of naïve enthusiasm. But the tendency to mobilize scattered fragments of ancient religious teachings has spread far beyond the borders of "Californialand" and is now having its effect within the very realm that scarcely a generation ago banished religion under the label of neurosis. A large and growing number of psychotherapists are now convinced that the Eastern religions offer an understanding of the mind far more complete than anything yet envisaged by Western science. At the same time, the leaders of the new religions themselves—the numerous gurus and spiritual teachers now in the West—are reformulating and adapting the traditional systems according to the language and atmosphere of modern psychology.

For example, in Berkeley, during the summers of 1973 and 1974, the Tibetan lama Tarthang Tulku led a six-week seminar in meditation exercises and Buddhist philosophy especially designed for professional psychologists. "What I mainly learned here," remarked one participant, "was how limited my concept of therapy had been. Ninety percent of what we are concerned with would be a joke to Rinpoche."* Another, a Freudian analyst from New York, left convinced that Tibetan Buddhism can reverse the "hardening of the arteries" which has afflicted the practice of psychoanalysis.

Yet another Tibetan teacher, Chögyam Trungpa, is working on an even larger scale in this direction and is now establishing a psychiatric center where ancient Tibetan methods will be mingled with modern psychotherapeutic techniques.

Taking his inspiration from elements of the Sufi tradition, psychologist Robert Ornstein writes:

> We are now for the first time in a position to begin seriously dealing with a psychology which can speak of a 'transcendence of time as we know it.' . . . These traditional psychologies have been relegated to the 'esoteric' or the 'occult,' the realm of the mysterious—the word most often employed is 'mysticism.'. . . For Western students of psychology and science, it is time to begin a new synthesis, to 'translate' some of the concepts and ideas of traditional psychologies into modern psychological terms, to regain a balance lost. To do this, we must first extend the boundaries of inquiry of modern science, *extend our concept of what is possible for man.*[1]

Space does not permit the mention of more than a fragment of all the activity and theorizing now taking place among psychiatrists and psychologists attracted to Zen and Tibetan Buddhism, Sufism, Hinduism in its numerous forms, and, lately, even the practices of early monastic and Eastern Christianity, as well as certain surviving remnants of the mystical Judaic tradition—Kabbalah and Hasidism. There is also the work of

* Tibetan for "teacher."

the humanistic and existentialist schools of psychology, pioneered by the researches of A. H. Maslow, which are converging their energies on the mystical, or, as they call it, "transpersonal," dimension of psychology. Studies of states of consciousness, peak experiences, biofeedback, the psychophysiology of yoga, and mind-expanding drugs are more often than not set within the context of ideas and systems that hark back to the ancient integrative sciences of man. Finally, there is the acceleration of interest in the teachings of Carl Jung, who from the very beginning moved away from the scientism of his mentor, Freud, and toward the symbols and metaphysical concepts of the esoteric and occult.

With all these disparate movements, it is no wonder that thousands of troubled men and women throughout America no longer know whether they need psychological or spiritual help. The line is blurred that divides the therapist from the spiritual guide. As one observer, speaking only half facetiously, put it, "The shrinks are beginning to sound like gurus, and the gurus are beginning to sound like shrinks."

But is it so easy to distinguish between the search for happiness and the search for transformation? Are psychotherapy and spiritual tradition simply two different approaches to the same goal, two different conceptions of what is necessary for well-being, peace of mind, and personal fulfillment? Or are they two quite separate directions that human life can take? What is the real difference between sacred tradition and psychotherapy?

Consider this fragment of an old Scottish fairy tale attributed to the pre-Christian Celts. It tells of two brothers meeting on the side of an enchanted mountain. One is climbing the mountain and the other is descending. One is being led upward by a miraculous crane, to which he is attached by a long golden thread. The other is led downward by a snarling black dog straining at an iron chain. They stop to speak about their journey and compare their difficulties. Each describes the same sorts of dangers and obstacles—precipices, huge sheer boulders, wild animals—and the same pleasures—wondrous vistas, beautiful, fragrant flowers. They agree to continue their journey together, but immediately the crane pulls the first brother upward and the dog drags the second downward. The first youth cuts the golden thread and seeks to guide himself upward solely by what he has heard from the other. But although all the obstacles are exactly as the second brother has indicated, he finds them unexpectedly guarded by evil spirits, and without the crane to guide him he is constantly driven back and is himself eventually transformed into a spirit who must eternally stand guard inside a gaping crevasse.

The larger context of this tale is not known, but it may serve very well to open the question of the relationship between psychiatry and the sacred. Of all the numerous legends, fairy tales, and myths that concern what are called "the two paths of life" (sometimes designated "the path of the fall" and "the path of the return"), this particular fragment uniquely focuses on a neglected point about the differences between the obstacles to awakening and the obstacles to happiness. The tale is saying that however similar the obstacles to these two aims might appear, in actuality they are very different. And woe to him who fails to take into account both possible movements of the inner life of man. Woe to him who does not attend to both the divinity and the animal in himself. He will never move either toward earthly happiness *or* toward self-transformation.

This tale almost seems specifically designed to expose our present uncertainty about so-called spiritual psychology. Consider the ideas emanating from ancient Eastern traditions that are now entering into the stream of modern psychological language: ideas about states of consciousness, enlightenment, meditation, freedom from the ego, self-realization—to name only a few. Is it possible that each of these terms can be understood from two different angles of vision? For example, does one meditate in order to resolve the problems of life or to become conscious of the automatic movement of forces in oneself?

Our question concerns psychiatry considered as a means to an end, as the removal of obstacles that stand in the way of happiness. (I choose the word *happiness* only for the sake of brevity; we could equally well speak of the goal of psychiatry as useful living, the ability to stand on one's own feet, or adjustment to society.) These obstacles to happiness—our fears, unfulfilled desires, violent emotions, frustrations, maladaptive behavior—are the sins of our modern psychiatric religion. But now we are asked to understand that there exist teachings about the universe and about man under whose guidance the psychological obstacles, these sins against happiness, may be accepted and studied as material for the development of the force of consciousness.

Perhaps at this point it would be helpful to pause briefly and reflect upon the general idea of the transmutation of consciousness. The word *"consciousness"* is used nowadays in so many different senses that it is tempting to single out one or another aspect of consciousness as its primary characteristic. The difficulty is compounded by the fact that our attitude toward knowledge about ourselves is like our attitude toward new discoveries about the external world. We so easily lose our balance when something extraordinary is discovered in science or when we come upon an exciting new explanatory concept: immediately the whole machinery of systematic thought comes into play. Enthusiasm sets in, accompanied by a proliferation of utilitarian explanations, which then stand in the way of direct encounters with the real, moving world.

In a like manner, a new experience of the self tempts us to believe we have discovered the sole direction for the development of consciousness, aliveness, or—as it is sometimes called—presence. The same machinery of explanatory thought comes into play, accompanied by pragmatic programs for action. It is not only followers of the new religions who may fall victim to this tendency, taking fragments of traditional teachings which have brought them a new experience of themselves and building a religion around them. This tendency in ourselves also accounts for much of the fragmentation of modern psychology, just as it accounts for fragmentation in the natural sciences.

In order to call attention to this tendency in ourselves, the traditional teachings—as in the *Bhagavad Gita,* for example—make a fundamental distinction between *consciousness* and the *contents of consciousness.* In the light of this distinction, everything we ordinarily take to be consciousness (or our real self) is actually identified as the *contents of consciousness*: our perceptions of things, our sense of personal identity, our emotions, and our thoughts in all their colors and gradations.

This ancient distinction has two crucial messages for us. On the one hand, it tells us that what we feel to be the best of ourselves as human beings is only part of a total structure containing layers of mind, feeling, and sensation far more active, subtle, and unifying than what we have settled for as our best. These layers are incredibly numerous and need to be peeled back, as it were, one by one along the path of inner growth (the upward path of our tale) until one touches in oneself the fundamental intelligent force in the cosmos.

At the same time, this distinction also communicates that the awakening of consciousness requires a constant effort. It is telling us that anything in ourselves, no matter how subtle, fine, or intelligent, no matter how close to reality or virtuous, no matter how still or violent—any action, any thought, any intuition or experience—immediately devours our attention and becomes automatically transformed into *contents,* around which gather all the opinions, feelings, and distorted sensations that are the supports of our secondhand sense of identity. In short, we are told that the evolution of man is always (eternally) vertical to the downward-flowing stream of mental, emotional, and physical associations within the human psyche. The downward pull of gravity is within ourselves. And seen in this light, there are no concentric layers of human awareness that need to be peeled back like the skins of an onion, but only one skin, one veil, that is constantly forming regardless of the quality of the psychic field at any given moment.

From this latter perspective, the main requirement for understanding the nature of consciousness is the repeated *effort* to be aware of whatever is taking place in the whole of ourselves at any given moment. All definitions or systematic explanations, no matter how profound, are secondary. Thus teachings about consciousness, both of the ancient masters and of modern psychologists, can be a distraction if they are presented to us in a way that does not support the effort to be aware of the totality of ourselves in the present moment.

In traditional cultures special terms surround this quality of self-knowledge, connecting it to the direct human participation in a higher, all-encompassing reality, "beyond the Earth," as it is sometimes said. The existence of these special terms, such as *satori* (Zen Buddhism), *fana* (Islam), *pneuma* (Christianity), and many others, may serve for us as a sign that this effort of total awareness was always set apart from the normal, everyday goods of organized social life. And while the traditional teachings tell us that any human being may engage in the search for this quality of presence, it is ultimately recognized that only very few will actually wish to do so, for it is a struggle that in the last analysis is undertaken solely for its own sake, without recognizable psychological motivation. And so, imbedded within every traditional culture there is said to be an esoteric or inner path discoverable only by those who yearn for something inexplicably beyond the duties and satisfactions of religious, intellectual, moral, and social life.

What we can recognize as psychiatric methods in traditional cultures must surely be understood in this light. Psychosis and neurosis were obviously known to the ancient world just as they are known in the few remaining traditional societies that still exist today in scattered pockets throughout the world. In a traditional culture, then, the challenge of what we would call psychotherapy consisted in bringing a person back to a normal life without stamping out the nascent impulse toward transformation in the process of treatment. To do this, a practitioner would have had to recognize the difference in a man between thwarted normal psychological functioning and the unsatisfied yearning ("that comes from nowhere," as one Sufi teacher has described it) for the evolution of consciousness. Certainly, that is one reason why traditionally the psychotic was treated by the priest. It is probably also why what we would call neurosis was handled within the once-intact family structure, permeated as this structure was by the religious teachings of the culture.

It has been observed that modern psychiatry could have assumed its current place only after the breakdown of the traditional family structure that dates back to the beginnings of recorded history. But the modern psychiatrist faces a tremendously difficult task as a surrogate parent even beyond the problems that have been so thoroughly described under the psychoanalytic concept of transference. For there may be something far deeper, subtler, and more intensely human, something that echoes of a cosmic dimension, hidden behind the difficulties and therapeutic opportunities of the classical psychoanalytic transference situation. We have already given this hidden something a name: the desire for self-transformation. In the ancient traditional family structure (as I am told it still exists, for example, among the Brahmin families of India) the problems of living a normal, fulfilled life are never separated from the sense of a higher dimension of human existence. What we might recognize as therapeutic counseling is given by family members or friends, but in such a way that a troubled individual will never confuse the two possible directions that his life can take. He is helped to see that the obstacles to happiness are not necessarily the obstacles to spiritual realization, as it is called in such traditions. A great many of what we take to be intolerable restrictions—such as predetermined marriage partners or vocations—are connected to this spiritual factor in the make-up of the traditional patterns of family life.

Can the modern psychiatrist duplicate this aspect of family influence? Almost certainly, he cannot. For one thing, he himself probably did not grow up in such a family milieu; almost none of us in the modern world have. Therefore, the task he faces is even more demanding than most of us realize. He may recognize that religion has become a destructive influence in people's lives because the path of transformation offered by the traditions has become covered over by ideas and doctrines we have neither understood nor experienced. He may even see that this same process of getting lost in undigested spiritual ideas and methods is taking place among many followers of the new religions. But at the same time, perhaps he sees that there can exist in people—be they neurotic or normal—this hidden desire for inner evolution. How can the patient be led to a normal, happy life without crushing this other, hidden impulse that can bring human life into a radically different dimension—whether or not a person ever becomes happy or self-sufficient or adjusted in the usual sense of these words? For the development of consciousness in man may not necessarily entail the development of what would be called a normal, well-adjusted, or self-sufficient personality.

Let us now look more closely at the process of modern psychotherapeutic healing against the background of the ancient, traditional understanding of human nature.

We may begin with the idea of levels of unity within the human organism. Both the spiritual guide and the therapist come upon the individual existing in a state of hidden fragmentation and dispersal. A man cannot be what he wishes to be. His behavior, his feelings, his very thoughts bring him pain or, what is even worse, an endless round of empty satisfactions and unconfronted terrors. As it is said, "he does not know who he is." The sense of identity that society and his upbringing have thrust upon him does not square with what he feels to be his instincts, his gut-level needs, and his deepest aspirations. He is constantly fleeing from loneliness or boredom, states in which there is nothing or no one to confirm his identity through the stimulation of desire.

Beneath the fragile sense of personal identity, the individual is actually an innumerable swarm of disconnected impulses, thoughts, reactions, opinions, and sensations, which are triggered into activity by causes of which he is totally unaware. Yet at each moment, the individual identifies himself with whichever of this swarm of impulses and reactions happens to be active, automatically affirming each as "himself," and then taking a stand either for or against this "self," depending on the particular pressures that the social environment has brought to bear upon him since childhood.

The traditions identify this affirming-and-denying process as the real source of human misery and the chief obstacle to the development of man's inherent possibilities. Through this affirmation and denial a sort of form is constructed around each of the passing impulses originating in the different parts of the human organism. And this continuous, unconscious affirmation of identity traps a definite amount of precious psychic energy in a kind of encysting process that is as much chemical-biological as it is psychological. The very nerves and muscles of the body are called upon to defend and support the affirmation of "I" around each of the countless groups of impulses and reactions as they are activated.

Several years ago, when I was moderating a seminar of psychiatrists and clinicians, the real dimensions of this affirmation process were brought home in a very simple and powerful way. We were all discussing the use of hypnosis in therapy, and the question arose as to what actually takes place in hypnosis, and what it means that human beings are in general hypnotizable. At some point during the discussion one of the participants began to speak in a manner that riveted everyone's attention. He was a psychoanalyst, the oldest and most respected member present.

"Only once in my life," he said, "did I ever use hypnosis with a patient. It was in the Second World War, when I was in the Swiss Army. There was this poor soldier in front of me, and for some reason I decided

to test whether or not he would be susceptible to posthypnotic suggestion. I easily brought him into a trance and, simply by way of experiment, I suggested to him that after he awoke he would stamp his foot
three times whenever I snapped my fingers. All perfectly standard pro-
cedure. After I brought him out of the trance state and we spoke for a
while, I dismissed him, and just as he was leaving the room I snapped
my fingers. He immediately responded and stamped his foot according
to the suggestion. 'Wait a minute,' I shouted. 'Tell me, why did you
stamp your foot?' His face suddenly turned beet red. 'Damn it all,' he
said, 'I've got something in my shoe.' "

The speaker slowly puffed on his pipe and his face became extremely
serious. The rest of us could not understand why he seemed to be making so much of this well-known phenomenon of posthypnotic fabrica-
tion. But he maintained his silence, staring somberly down the length of
his pipe. No one else said a word—it was obvious that he was trying to
formulate something that he took to be quite important. Then, with his
face suddenly as open as a child's, he looked up at me, and said, "Do you
think the whole of our psychic life is like that?"

A strange and rather awkward silence followed. Some of the company
obviously felt that this man, whom everyone acknowledged as a great
practitioner, was having a temporary intellectual lapse. But the others,
myself included, were struck by the extraordinary feeling he had put
into this simple question, as though he were at that very moment inter-
nally revising everything he had ever understood about the mind.

Everyone was looking at me, waiting for me to reply. And, in fact,
what he was driving at had already dawned on me. But before I could
speak, he went on in exactly the same way except that his face now regis-
tered not only amazement, but something akin to horror:

"Do you think," he said, "that every movement we make, every word
we say, every thought we have is like that? Could it be that we are always 'fabricating' in a sort of low-grade posthypnotic haze? Because
there's one thing I am sure of, though only now do I see its importance:
the moment I asked that soldier why he had stamped his foot, there was
a split second when he realized that *he* had not *done* anything at all. A
moment when he realized that the fact was simply that his foot stamped
the ground 'all by itself.' By asking him why he had stamped his foot, I
was in effect suggesting to his mind that *he* had *done* something. In short,
I was still hypnotizing him—or, rather, I was playing into the general
process of hypnosis that is going on all the time with all of us from the
cradle to the grave. The contradiction made him blush, and the true
facts about the foot-stamping were blotted out of awareness."

Another silence, very brief. Some of the other participants were nearly bursting with impatience to have their say. But I chose not to recognize anyone else. I was totally fascinated with where the thought of this speaker was taking him. He went on for quite a while, weaving his speculations around the possibility that the whole of man's psychic life is the product of suggestions coming from different sources, some immediately external and others stored in the mechanisms of memory. And this whole process, he concluded, is constantly screened from our awareness by the belief, also conditioned into us, that we are acting, individual selves. Our so-called freedom of the will is only an *ex post facto* identification with processes that are taking place "all by themselves."

From earlier conversations with this psychiatrist, I knew he had never gone very deeply into the study of spiritual traditions, not even Western traditions. He knew nothing about the Buddhist diagnosis of the human condition as permeated by the delusion of selfhood. He was totally unfamiliar with the ancient Pythagorean symbolism of reincarnation. In that symbolism the psyche (or soul) that does not progress toward the evolution of consciousness is said to reincarnate into lower forms of life (such as animals). As in the Buddhist teaching, this image of reincarnation symbolizes the prison of identifying with partial and automatic psychic processes, to the extent that the whole energy of the psyche is more and more encysted or trapped within a narrow range of psychological postures, repeating over and over again, for endless eons.

What, then, is the picture we have before us?

Through social custom, through education, through the indoctrinations and influences of religion, art, and family, the individual is made to accept at a very early age that he is an integral whole, persisting through time, possessing a real identity and a definite psychic structure. Yet as an adult, he is actually a thousand loosely connected psychophysical cysts. As he leaves childhood and affirms this socially conditioned identity, he is actually leaving behind the possible growth of his inner structure. The evolution of a true psychic integrity comes to a halt, requiring, as it does, the very energy that is now diverted and consumed in upholding the sense of "I." The individual becomes a lie, a lie that is now ingrained in the very neural pathways of the organism. He habitually, automatically pretends he is one and whole—it is demanded of him and he demands it of himself. Yet in fact he is scattered and multiple.

But he cannot help himself now. It is useless to throw moral imperatives at him. For there is no ruling principle within him and thus nothing that could change the course of his inner condition. All the knowledge, experience, and impressions that are meant to nourish the development of the inner psychic structure with which he was born are either sloughed off and grounded, or absorbed in distorted fashion solely to support the hidden affirmation process. A man lives in his own world, as it is said. The sensitive current of feeling that is meant to permeate the entire being as an indispensable organ of knowledge and will is now channeled instead into the emotions of the ego—such as fear, self-satisfaction, self-pity, and competitiveness. Blended with the extremely volatile and combinative energies of sex, these emotions become so pervasive that they are accepted as the real nature of man, as his unconscious or his animal nature, the reality behind the appearances.

And it is true. These emotions and drives, now fueled and maintained by stealing the energies of the sexual nature, are pervasive and all-powerful. And yet, in a deeper sense, it is not true. For these emotions are only powerful in the formation and maintenance of the affirmation-and-negation process that screens the basic fragmentation of the human psyche. In the traditional understanding, the real unconscious is the hidden psychic integrity, which has been forgotten and left behind in childhood, and which requires for its development not egoistic satisfactions, not recognition from others, not sexual or libidinal pleasure, not even physical security, food, and shelter. This original face of man requires only the energy of truth—that is to say, the real impressions of the external and internal world carried to the embryonic essence of man by means of the faculty of free attention. Thus, according to tradition, there is something potentially divine within man, which is born when his physical body is born but which needs for its growth an entirely different sustenance from what is needed by the physical body or the social self.

Traditionally, then, the term *self-knowledge* has an extraordinary meaning. It is neither the acquisition of information about oneself nor a deeply felt insight nor moments of recognition against the ground of psychological theory. It is an act that is in itself the principal means by which the evolving part of man can be nourished with an energy that is as real, or more so, as the energy delivered to the physical organism by the food we eat. Thus it is not a question of acquiring strength, independence, self-esteem, security, meaningful relationships, or any of the other goods upon which the social order is based and which have been identified as the components of psychological health. It is solely a matter of digesting deep impressions of myself as I actually am from moment to moment: a disconnected, helpless collection of impulses and reactions, a being of disharmonized mind, feeling, and instinct.

I should like to conclude by asking my question from a slightly different angle. Both among psychiatrists and the general public a widespread sense of crisis has set in concerning the psychological condition of man on this planet. Accelerated changes in the patterns of social life and the threats of war and overdeveloped technology are now more and more being met by the unleashing of powerful ideas torn from the traditional integrative sciences of man, against the background of the swift modernization of traditional cultural environments throughout the world. The mixture of these forces has induced a combination of fear and a visionary mentality concerning the possible evolution of planetary and individual man.

Yet in the private lives of almost everyone these same forces of scientific advance and cultural homogenization continue to produce painful and dehumanizing effects on the quality of our lived experience. The passive acceptance of scientific concepts of time, space, energy—and lately of mind—drives man further and further away from discovering his own space, his own time, his own vital energy, and his own active intelligence. So connected to the species has the individual become that his patterns of thought and feeling are now dictated on a worldwide basis by the needs and sufferings of the biological organism, man-on-earth.

Lost in all this is the human middle zone between the creature of earth and the private universe called "atman" in the Hindu traditions, "spirit" in Christianity, or simply "myself," "I," my original face. This middle zone of human life was once known as the family, the community, the tribe. Through the conditions of family life, the development and interiorization of the self could take place alongside the growth of the individual as a cell in the body of man-on-earth. The middle zone of human life was the product of a religion in which both heaven and earth, as ideas and as possible dimensions of living, could be the everyday environment of human life. The exaggerated influence of scientism destroyed this two-natured environment quite as decisively as it now threatens to destroy the environment of biological man. Against this former, more fundamental environmental destruction, modern psychiatry arose to help bring man back into contact with the life of feeling, a life that at the turn of the century was already being obliterated by dogmatic, intercultural religion, religion also cut off from the middle zone of human life, religion become worldly in the sense of being homogeneous, doctrinaire, and explanatory. In international Christianity, the church lost contact with the hidden existence in man of an embryonic yearning for the external and instead imposed beliefs and explanatory concepts patterned after the species-and-survival knowledge of modern science. In the present era the centuries-long process was completed by which the Christian religion surrendered its ancient quiet influence on the heart of man and gave itself up instead to persuading, arguing, and compelling radical choices on a being in whom the decision to seek for oneself does not have to be *made* but only *heard.*

In the nineteenth and twentieth centuries the concept of mysticism was developed in order to classify a part of the self that science could not explain. Later, the same forces that classified mysticism eventually defined the mind, and, as we have said, the mind became an object of scientific exploration. Mysticism was pushed even further aside while the mind as a whole was naturalized—that is, understood as part of the biological organism. That there is such a mind, which functions as part of the biological organism, was always known and given various names in the traditional teachings; disturbances of this physical, biological mind, the species mind, were always treated by the traditional physician-priests, whose task it was to distinguish the sufferings of the physical mind from the yearnings for growth that emanated from the private mind, or soul.

Today, however, with the influx of fragments of traditional teachings and with the current disillusionment in the sciences, techniques for treating the physical mind of man are being joined without real guidance to ideas and methods that pertain to the individual, private mind that was always understood to be rooted in another level of reality—a mind, a consciousness, that is said to have a life independent of the motivations that constitute the ego of the human being.

At the heart of the great traditions is the idea that the search for truth is undertaken for its own sake ultimately. These traditional teachings in their entirety propose to show man the nature of this search and the laws behind it—laws which, as I have suggested, too often get lost in our enthusiasm for ideas and explanations that we have not deeply absorbed in the fire of living with all its suffering and confusion. Psychotherapy, on the other hand, is surely a *means* to an end—to the goal we have called happiness. Unlike the way offered by tradition, therapy is never an end in itself, never a way of life, but is motivated toward a goal that the therapist sees more clearly than his patient. The therapist may even experiment with invented methods to achieve this goal and often succeeds. But is it recognized that two kinds of success are possible in the process of therapy? On the one hand, the successful result may be a patient in whom the wish for evolution has been totally disillusioned and stamped out through the deliberate arousal in himself of the very quality of egoistic emotion which the traditions seek to break down and dissolve. But another kind of success may be possible in certain cases—a patient in whom the wish for evolution has been driven inside, who no longer dreams of a response to this wish from the outside world, but who now has within him an even greater sensitivity and hunger for deeper contact with himself. To the outside observer, such a person may seem to have developed a certain inner-directedness, but in actuality he is precisely the sort of person who may desperately need what the traditions seek to communicate. The effort of contemporary teachers from the East to bring their message to such people in terms that are neither freighted with dead antiquity nor compromised by modern psychologisms consti- tutes the real spiritual drama of the present age.

I suspect that psychiatrists sense there can be these two different kinds of success in the process of psychotherapy. But the second class of pa- tients probably leave the therapist before the treatment is far advanced, while the first class of patients stay in treatment as long as they can. Therefore, this second type of patient is probably not consciously or of- ficially recognized by the profession of psychiatry.

So the question comes to this: in the personal crisis of my life, what sort of help do I seek? And the answer, in all sincerity, seems to revolve around the following fact. It is in the periods *between* crises that I reflect upon different paths and set up standards regarding whom I will trust and who has the truth about human nature. The point is that when I am in trouble it is not the spiritual guide or psychotherapist that I turn to. It is something in myself, a part of myself, that I turn to. Some ideas, some habits of thinking, some memories, some reports settled in my mind, some emotional associations: these are the guides that lead me. In the moment when life is crushing me, it may seem that I take any hand that is offered. But it is not true. I have an inner guide that leads me.

Of course, it is extremely inaccurate to refer to this collection of chance associations and emotional impulses, this loose federation of fears, prejudices, and habitual patterns of self-suggestion, as an inner guide. It is an inaccurate phrase if by guide we mean someone or some- thing that leads us to the truth about ourselves. For, this inner guide knows nothing of truth. Moreover, it gives great-sounding names—such as transformation, freedom, and self-expression—only to experiences that conform to its chance requirements, its need for the illusion of unity, while the rest of my nature remains unknown and unintegrated. This inner guide is the ego. Yet the term *inner guide* is accurate in that it is actually what I turn to when facing both sacred tradition and psycho- therapy. It is what gets me through the night, and through my life.

Which of you, spiritual guides and psychotherapists, knows this aspect of my nature and its real place in my life? Which of you takes it into account when I ask for help? Which of you can hear the faint cry behind it of something in myself that wishes for truth? And which of you can address both sides of my nature, these two sides that we are told are created in man to struggle with each other so that out of this struggle a new being, a real *I*, can be born. For the "third brother"—so the traditions tell us—can only come into being and move forward out of the struggle between the other two.

I see, therefore, that in the last analysis the names "spiritual guide" and "psychotherapist" are not the essential thing. I see that even the ideas and methods offered me by a spiritual teacher can be taken over by my egoistic inner guide and used to take me only toward the lesser unities of social happiness and independence. And what of the help offered me under the name of psychotherapy? Among you therapists, do there exist people who feel the two sides of human nature and are sensitive to their simultaneous claims, the possible struggle between them, the emergence within man of that middle world between heaven and earth in which—classically speaking, and using the ancient language of alchemy—good and evil, active and passive, masculine and feminine engage in a warfare that can discover the moment of internal love, an inner exchange of substance leading to the birth of the New Man?

Spiritual guides and psychotherapists, what do your names mean? How should we accept what you call yourselves? Behind these names, which of you are the real spiritual guides and which the real psychotherapists? We need to know. I need to know.

REFERENCES

1. Robert E. Ornstein, *The Psychology of Consciousness* (San Francisco: W. H. Freeman, 1972), pp. 96–99.

THE TWO SCIENCES OF MEDICINE
Notes Toward an Understanding
of Medicine as a Sacred Science

Introduction: The Question

Whereas God created the physician . . . and appointed him to be useful
to other men, it is good for him to know, in order to accomplish such
special works, that he has no other duty but to drive out disease. If this
is his office, he must act like God, his Lord, who appointed him. God
took away the disease of the Great World (the macrocosm). . . . To take
away the diseases of the Little World (the microcosm), those of man, he
ordained the physician. If the physician is thus a god of the Little
World, appointed as God's deputy, on what foundation should he
build, and from whom shall he learn if not from the oldest physician,
from God? . . . If the physician understands things exactly and sees and
recognizes all illnesses in the macrocosm outside man, and if he has a
clear idea of man and his whole nature, then and only then is he a physician. Then he may approach the inside of man; then he may examine
his urine, take his pulse, and understand where each thing belongs. . . .
Just as a man can see himself reflected exactly in a mirror, so the physician must have exact knowledge of man and recognize him in the mirror of the four elements, in which the whole microcosm reveals itself.

The physician should speak of that which is invisible. What is visible
should belong to his knowledge, and he should recognize the illnesses,
just as everybody else, who is not a physician, can recognize them by
their symptoms. But this is far from making him a physician; he becomes a physician only when he knows that which is unnamed, invisible, and immaterial, yet efficacious.

. . . Medical science . . . is full of mysteries, and must be studied like the
words of Christ.[1]

THE writings of the incomparable sixteenth-century physician and
alchemist Paracelsus are invaluable to us if we would inquire about

medicine as an ancient and sacred science, thereby reaching for a fresh
perspective from which to view both the spectacular successes and failures of modern medical science. Never forgetting, of course, that our
main aim is to look for a bridge between the great knowledge of the archaic past and the exigencies of the present.

Addressing his fellow physicians, Paracelsus writes further:

> Health and sickness are granted by God; nothing comes from man. . . .
> You should divide the diseases of men . . . into those which arise in a
> natural way, and those which come upon us as God's scourges. For take
> good note of it: God has sent us some diseases as a punishment, as a
> warning, as a sign by which we know that all our affairs are naught, that
> our knowledge rests upon no firm foundation, and that the truth is not
> known to us, but that we are inadequate and fragmentary in all ways,
> and that no ability or knowledge is ours.[2]

I think it is well to begin our discussion with these passages, which
may strike the modern mind as not only fanciful, but outrageous. They
smack of superstition, false consolation, and the sort of passivity which
blocks effective action. Nevertheless, such thoughts must at one time or
another have crossed the minds of many persons who have suffered from
serious illness and many physicians whose sustained efforts to help have
failed.

As medicine struggled to find a place among the exact sciences in the
modern era, it quickly backed away from the idea that diseases have a
meaning. Just as science in general viewed the universe as a blind chain
of processes, so the body was also viewed in this way. Just as the mission
of science was to ascertain the laws of nature in order to intervene and
satisfy the desires of men, so medicine became progressively interven-
tional. While many individual doctors continued to rely in part on a sort
of intuition and on a general impulse to flow with nature intelligently in
times of physical crisis, the general trend of medicine was in the opposite
direction.

All of this was part of a general humanistic rejection of the idea that
man is weak and helpless before the great forces of nature. But in the
modern era the traditional notion of man's helplessness had become
badly misinterpreted. In the ancient teachings it is held that the more
man sees of his weakness, the more possible it becomes for a greater force
to work through him. In this sense, sin is the tendency of man willfully to
remain established in a part of his being that by itself cannot receive
greater energy.

This is an extremely important consideration that can help us break away from what appear to be naïve religious-medical formulations in the Western Bible. Expressed in the language of religion, God cannot give to man unless man actively seeks to receive from God. A too literal reading of scripture makes it sound as though diseases are sometimes punishments for disobedience, just as we angrily punish a naughty child. But from the point of view we shall be examining, a scourge from God, or anything else from God, only comes to a man who is searching for God—searching, that is, for a greater understanding of his life and a surer contact with higher forces. In short, disease—as well as any other event in life—has meaning only to men in search of meaning.

1. Disease and Meaning

The ecological crisis has taught us that we have been wrong to approach the surrounding world as would-be conquerors, manipulating nature only in order to satisfy all our desires and fears. Carrying our technological discoveries to excess, we provoke from nature responses which now begin to terrify us and which lead us to reconsider the whole metaphysical foundation of modern science.

But what of our bodies? Have we not approached the body in the same way we have approached the universe—as conquerors? For example, is the overuse of antibiotics, as some have claimed, like the abuse of pesticides? the excessive reliance on radical surgery like the plundering of forests, minerals, and animal species for the sake of short-term gain? the constant turning to drugs for symptomatic or emotional relief like the massive diversion of natural energy resources for physical comfort and ease? It would be intellectually very gratifying to say yes to this and to be able to point to the medical equivalent of all the various ecological crises that now face us. But it is not so simple. External nature apparently draws the picture of our errors much more obviously, with a much bigger brush, than does our own body. The truth seems to be that we really do not know what we are doing to our bodies. We do not even know what the body is for.

In order to approach this difficult subject, I would like to ask some questions about the science of medicine as such. They may sound foolish to physicians or knowledgeable historians of medicine. But I'm sure questions like these are troubling many others who are hearing more and more about such nonorthodox medical approaches as homeopathy, acupuncture, herbal medicine, and psychic healing.

To start with there is the whole matter of the origins of modern medi-

cine and the supposed abysmal ignorance of all those who went before.
In the year 1543 Nicolaus Copernicus published the epoch-making
work, *On the Revolution of Celestial Orbs,* the first modern, mathematical
statement of the heliocentric theory. In the same year a remarkable
young Belgian professor of anatomy, Andreas Vesalius, published *On the
Fabric of the Human Body.* Famed as the first real anatomical text based on
direct observation of the human cadaver, it contains a series of magnificent illustrations of the skeletal, muscular, vascular, and neural structure
of the body as a whole. According to the eminent historian of medicine,
Charles Singer,

> The masterpiece of Vesalius is not only the foundation of modern medi-
> cine as a science, but the first great positive achievement of science itself
> in modern times.... The work of Copernicus removed the Earth from
> the center of the Universe; that of Vesalius revealed the real structure of
> man's body.[3]

Now let us hear what another historian of medicine says about the period preceding the birth of modern medicine in the Renaissance:

> The period between modern and ancient times (includes) a period of
> roughly a millenium. During most of these years, civilization was
> dragged down to a low level and mankind, hopelessly restricted by the
> authority of the Church, frittered away its existence with war and mo-
> nastic dreams.

> From the fifth to the eleventh century little progress was made in Eu-
> rope. This epoch, often referred to as the Dark Ages, was a period in
> history when the higher ideals of European learning were relegated to a
> very base position.... Both secular and independent learning de-
> teriorated but the greatest stagnation took place in the fields of philoso-
> phy and medicine.[4]

These are by no means exceptional quotations. Almost every historical study of Western medicine gives us a picture of medieval man stag-
gering for a thousand years under the weight of blind, ineffectual superstition about disease and the functions of the human body.

I have neither the knowledge nor the wish to dispute the common
opinion that during the Christian Middle Ages medical superstition was
rampant and that there was very little in the way of experimental verifi-
cation in these matters. But a thousand years is a very long time and
many extraordinary people existed during that period. Forty generations of human beings were born, lived, and died; they all had bodies

and suffered pain and disease. Are we to believe that the greatest intellects of the Christian era were the pawns of blind superstition about the human body? Even the sharpest critics of the Middle Ages allow that effective remedies of many different kinds abounded and that the immediate concern of the medically trained monks was the relief of their patients' suffering. What is condemned is the lack of scientific observation and theory as we know it. Then we may ask, did the traditions perhaps shelter another kind of study of the body which we do not even recognize or dignify with the name of knowledge?

It is all part of a larger question: what is it *necessary* to know about the body? Why has medicine always been associated with religion and what we now call magic? Do we really wish to maintain that mankind has been submerged in medical superstition in all epochs and in all cultures with the exception of our own? For let it be noted that even Hippocrates and his school, universally acknowledged as the ancient forerunner of modern empirical medicine, was Pythagorean. To the extent that we trust honest, though external, scholarship in this matter, the famous Hippocratic Oath has been persuasively shown to be a document of fourth-century B.C. Pythagoreanism. And among the many intriguing elements in this oath is the indication that in the school of Hippocrates medicine was taught in a manner resembling the transmission of spiritual knowledge from master to pupil.[5]

In the Hippocratic Oath the first thing to which the physician must swear is "To hold him who has taught me this art as equal to my parents and to live my life in partnership with him." This phrase, coupled with what we may surmise about the spiritual discipline of the Pythagorean school, forces us to reformulate our question. We ask not only what is necessary to know about the body, but what *kind* of learning is required? In connection with this, we may cite an account of medical education among the ancient Hindus. The author here is the noted Orientalist Heinrich Zimmer. "Hindu medical lore," he writes, "has been handed down through generations, not by faculties and bodies, colleges or research centers":

> It is the individual transference, as much as learning and being trained to use learning, that counts in the Hindu educational system. Through the intimate personal contact between master and pupil, living for years together in the master's household . . . the master infuses, as it were, the secret of his personal proficiency and mastery into him. Some kind of transformation is worked on the very substance of the obedient pupil. He has to be turned . . . into a new vessel which may be filled with the

wisdom and the skill of the teacher, and with the ancient spiritual inheritance transmitted through him. It is in this way that true master-
ship, according to Hindu belief, is handed down through the ages.[6]

This, of course, does not help us very much to understand what kind
of learning was required for the transmission of specifically medical
knowledge. It only tells us that mastery of the craft of medicine was intimately bound up with mastery of the sacred teachings, which is to say,
mastery of oneself. All the crafts of ancient India, Zimmer goes on to say,
were taught in this way and were never meant to serve purely utilitarian
or even aesthetic ends. A person became a craftsman—whether a silver-
smith, a carpenter, or a physician—only to the extent that he worked toward the perfection of his own inner being. The outer product, utilitarian though it was, was a result of the inner product, which we may call
the formation of a new consciousness. I think it is along these lines that
we may begin to understand the meaning of sacred art and crafts in traditional societies, and not simply in terms of the aesthetic characteristics
of the final product, important though that is.

Are we on the track of discovering the real difference between ancient
and modern medicine? Is what seems to us unscientific and crude in
early medical systems only a reflection of the difference between science
as we understand it today and craft as it was understood in traditional
societies? And, importantly enough, were these early physicians good
physicians? Unfortunately, it is hard to answer that question because
we, at least I, am not so sure what defines a good physician. It is a question many people are now asking, including quite a few concerned physicians themselves.

On this question, the Hindu tradition provides an interesting direction for our thinking. Zimmer recounts a seventeenth-century allegorical drama that summarizes the traditional point of view on the place
in the whole of human life of the craft of medicine. It is a long tale, but
pertinent to our question, and so I should like to present Zimmer's account with a few elements omitted and with a few rephrasings for the
sake of clarity.

The setting is the human organism. The kingdom of disease under its
king, Consumption, assails the royal capital of the body. *Jiva**, king of
the body, is to be driven from his realm.

---

* There is no really satisfactory English translation for this term which is so crucial in the
Hindu conception of man. Perhaps the best synonym in the present context is "the individual I."

The commander-in-chief of the army of diseases, Jaundice, heir to the throne, assembles the diseases of every sort for a council of war. The sixty-four diseases of the eye, the eighteen diseases of the nose and ears, the seventy-four diseases of the mouth, and the five diseases of the heart gather round him. These, however, form but a small part of the vast array.

Goiter, as master of ceremonies, opens the debate. Leprosy and Insanity make confident speeches. Boils and Ulcers show bold assurance, and so do the Piles and Urinary Diseases, including Diabetes, as well as the Stones. The host of Dysenteries, vaunting their disastrous impact, get full credit for their efficacy in breaking through the defenses of the enemy's body, while the Enlargements of the Spleen boast of their malignant effects, once they have gained access to the enemy's fortress.

Meanwhile a spy, Root of the Ear, has returned from King Jiva's realm, after having gathered intelligence disguised as a mendicant ascetic. The kingdom of Jiva is already besieged with diseases, he reports. But the king has retired to the innermost fortress of the body, having entered the inner citadel of the heart through the gate of the mind. There he approaches Lady Bhakti (loving devotion to God) in the hope that she will appeal to Siva (God) to grant the king the elixir of immortality, mercury, which is the very seed of God and the cure of all diseases.

The commanders of the army of diseases plot together on how to disorganize and disrupt the order of the king's household. For King Jiva himself is wholly inactive; he depends entirely on his active and circumspect chancellor, Intelligence, who represents extraverted consciousness which wisely attends to the things of the world.

During the crisis, this chancellor has ousted his rival, Spiritual Wisdom, who is unconcerned about worldly matters and to whom the passive king is all too ready to listen. The commanders of the army of diseases consider ways of reinstating Spiritual Wisdom with the king. Being wholly devoted to transcendental truth, his renewed influence could effectively block the strategies of the chancellor who is now managing the whole work of defense. But there are also other possibilities to consider. The chancellor's staff could be disrupted. His main functionaries, the three Humours (the body's principle organizing forces) could be upset by wrong diet or by drugs, both of which upset the proper balance of the Humours. Or perhaps the Mind, who is under the supervision of Worldly Intelligence, could be thwarted in his attempts to look after the welfare of the king. Fickle by nature, the Mind could easily be distracted by means of the pleasures and pains transmitted through the senses. In-

deed, the prospects look excellent for victory by the army of diseases and
for the banishment of King Jiva from his domain.

Meanwhile, in the innermost sanctuary of the heart, King Jiva and
Lady Bhakti have offered their worship to Siva. Siva bestows upon him
the powerful drugs of mercury and sulphur which, blended with medici-
nal herbs, bestow everlasting youth. The king quickly returns to the battlefield of his body, assured of the constant support of Lady Bhakti. The
commanders of the attacking armies realize that now that the king is
fortified with divine drugs they can only succeed if the king becomes estranged from devotion to God and also from his chancellor, Worldly Intelligence. The six Evil Passions, therefore, have sneaked into his realm
to cause disturbance—Lust, Greed, Anger, Hypocrisy, Envy, and Madness. But Discernment, the king's chief of police, sees through their dis-
guises and has them captured.

However, the king, now underestimating the peril which still menaces
his kingdom, turns too much of his attention to Lady Bhakti and becomes estranged from his chancellor. He lends a willing ear instead to
his other counsellor, Spiritual Wisdom, while Worldly Intelligence is
away inspecting the lines. Now, Spiritual Wisdom attends exclusively to
the transcendental. He distracts the king's attention from the city of the
body, directing his view to the mystery of his own higher essence, the im-
perishable divine principle of life which transcends this mortal coil. This
principle remains, forever and fundamentally, unconcerned with the
welfare or destruction of the physical or psychic shells which envelop the
individual I.

It takes utter disaster to bring the king to reason. A terrific assault by
the diseases, involving all forms of suffering, piercing shell after shell of
the organism, breaking through wall after wall, fortification after fortification, finally forces King Jiva to listen again to the advice of Worldly
Intelligence. Then the divine drugs, pharmaceutically prepared and
mobilized by the chancellor, arrive upon the battleground; in a pitched
battle, man to man, they conquer the entire army of diseases.

Broken, King Consumption quits the battlefield. Yet in a last-ditch
attempt, he hurls the group of incurable diseases in a surprise attack.
But in vain. Worldly Intelligence immediately advises the king to return
to Lady Bhakti for the practice of yoga meditation, even though her influence had previously been too great upon the king. But this time, Siva,
God, manifests himself to the king to bestow upon him the perfect wisdom of yoga, the true knowledge of the essence of God and the self,
which removes the king from all suffering and lifts him beyond all mortal cares. The king experiences the beatific identity of God with the in-

nermost core of man's nature. Finally, Siva imparts to King Jiva this teaching:

> Do not cease striving after the supreme enlightenment which bestows release from the bondage of the round of birth and death. Yet, at the same time, honor the wisdom of perfect worldly life and follow it. In giving to each sphere, the secular and spiritual, its due share, you will achieve both perfect enjoyment of earthly delights and final release. For only in so far as the city of the organism is maintained and firmly defended, can Yoga unfold its magic power to the fullest degree conducive to the plentitude of transcendental bliss.

Zimmer comments on how this drama (which is far more complex than here outlined) summarizes the vast material of the Hindu medical systems, physiology, dietetics, therapeutics, and so forth. But, he says, at the same time dramatic display of allegorical figures assigns to medical knowledge its proper place within the wider sphere of spiritual discipline which aims at the highest goal of man.

> It [the drama] seeks to coordinate the physician's and the layman's attention to physical well-being with the goals of faith, devotion, and yoga practice, the striving toward the beatific experience of the divine in human nature. Health, vigor, and longevity, though their possession naturally is of vital interest, do not constitute the self-sufficient ends of medical discipline. They are not ultimate values. They are subordinated to the higher goal of fulfillment on the transcendental plane. . . .

> This highest pursuit, the realization of man's metaphysical essence—that part of his nature which is supra-individual and indestructible—implies supreme indifference toward secular existence; yet, a fair balance is achieved here with regard to the claims of earthly individual existence: Worldly Intelligence and Lady Loving Devotion should share equally in the favor of King Jiva. . . .

> The moral of this medical allegory is that man must reconcile the antagonistic tendencies of his earthly individual nature and of his divine transcendent essence by satisfying the antithetical claims of both spheres, the natural and the supernatural: the phenomenal realm of body and psyche, and the imperishable essence which forms man's inherent being.[7]

It is true that the literature of the Christian Middle Ages seems to offer nothing comparable to this exact placing of the function of the medical art in terms of balancing the two natures of man. Nor am I aware of any indications in Medieval times of a school of medicine corresponding to the apparently Pythagorean school of Hippocrates in ancient Greece where, let us surmise, the craft of medicine was studied as an instrument of both inner development and external service. There are some who say the Benedictines and a few other monastic orders pursued medicine somewhat along these lines, but the general impression is that both within the monasteries and outside of them disease was looked upon as an affliction sent by God either to test man's soul or to punish him. If the Hindu drama urged men to attend wisely to their bodies for the sake of their soul, the Medieval Christian message was the reverse: man must not forget that all things, including health and illness, come from God and that in the last analysis only a right relationship to God can bring man any real good, physical or otherwise. Apparently, in the East cultural religious practices sought to correct the tendency of man to retreat into spirituality without caring rightly for the bodily nature. In the West, clearly, religious practices had the opposite task: to prevent man from attending to the body in such a way and with such an attitude that he forgot God. Excessive preoccupation with one's inner divinity was apparently not the central problem in the civilization of the West.

The perennial association of medicine and religion or magic throughout the ages must be understood in two ways. On the one hand, the craft of medicine was studied as a branch of the spiritual path, that is to say, as a means for self-perfection in the light of the teachings and disciplines of the spiritual path. On the other hand, medicine was studied and practiced at large as part of a culture's religion, that is to say, as one of the means for stabilizing and ordering the general life of a society. We shall return to this distinction which suggests that throughout the ages there has existed an inner and an outer side to the art of medicine.

But in order to think further about this whole subject it is first necessary to chase away or at least confront one demon in our own minds that stands in the way of finding a wider perspective. I mean the above-mentioned assumption about the vast superiority of modern medicine over anything that went before, and especially anything that existed in Medieval Europe. Many of us are willing to grant the great achievements in art, music, and architecture during the Christian Middle Ages, but as for medicine the strongest image we have is of epidemic and pestilence, particularly the Black Plague which in the fifteenth century is estimated to have wiped out twenty-five million people, roughly one-fourth of the entire population of Europe.

Our high estimation of modern medical science does rest largely on its success in combatting infectious epidemics. We in the modern, techno-

logically based world no longer stand in dread of plague, typhus, ty-
phoid fever, or other diseases which have ravaged Western civilization in
the past. But in one of the sanest books ever written about disease and
health, René Dubos has observed that "while modern science can boast
of so many startling achievements in the health fields, its role has not
been so unique and its effectiveness not so complete as is commonly
claimed." In reality, he writes,

> the monstrous specter of infection had become but an enfeebled shadow
> of its former self by the time serums, vaccines, and drugs became avail-
> able to combat microbes. Indeed, many of the most terrifying microbial
> diseases—leprosy, plague, typhus, and the sweating sickness, for exam-
> ple—had all but disappeared from Europe long before the advent of the
> germ theory.[8]

Equally important, our own apparently impressive longevity statistics
rest, Dubos tells us, on the marked decrease in infant mortality (due,
again, largely to improvement over nineteenth-century standards of nu-
trition, sanitation, and social conditions).

That is, more people grow to adulthood nowadays, so the average life-
span figures out arithmetically to be longer. But whether adults themselves enjoy better health or live longer is another question.

Moreover, we have our own epidemics and plagues, apart from the
obvious, recognizably infectious diseases. Future historians may well
look back upon our era and think of cancer, heart disease, hypertension,
and mental illness in much the way we think of the pestilences of the
Middle Ages.

Because of the modern attitude toward death, we tend to judge the effectiveness of medical science mainly in terms of prolongation of life in
the face of dramatic, acute mortal diseases. And, as we have seen, even
with this criterion, it is not certain that we are better off than our ancestors. But once we widen our criterion to include some of the other
countless factors involved in the meaning of health, our situation begins
to look even more questionable. It is true, Dubos observes, that we have
cleared away much of the filth and vermin that nurtured the killing diseases of the past few centuries. But, he writes, we are as much as ever
prey to illnesses "which do not take life, but just ruin it and which we
can neither diagnose nor cure." These chronic diseases, such as bron-
chitis, "do not have the blood-curdling character of the great pestilences
of the past." And for this reason they are often ignored in our thinking
about the successes of medicine. But Dubos argues that in terms of prev-

alence in our population and in terms of their indirect contributions to mortality, especially in older adults, many of them can be regarded as long-standing epidemics of the modern world.

And for every pathogenic microbe that we have for the time being controlled, there are other elements that we are introducing into our physical environment whose effects upon our health are as yet unmeasured or invisible: "we poison our atmosphere, and endanger future generations as well, with the gases of chemical processes, the smoke of factories, the pulverized rubber and exhaust of motor cars, and man-made radiations."

> Men are naturally most impressed by diseases which have obvious manifestations, yet some of their worst enemies creep on them unobtrusively. For example, any significant addition to background radiation increases the mutation rate of all life's creatures from plant to man, with results that will not be felt for several generations. And, likewise, the continuously mounting pollution of the air and the inescapable contact with drugs and chemicals that are becoming part of everyday life carry threats which are less obvious than cancer or heart disease but at least as important.[9]

It is not my intention to summarize all the considerations by which Dubos, himself a famous research physician, throws into question the common opinions about medical progress. He wrote this book several years before all of the sciences began to come under general suspicion, and now one could very well add to his list of factors: for example, he does not even mention what is called iatrogenic diseases, diseases caused by medical treatment itself, which are ranked third in importance among all the recognized ailments of contemporary man; nor does he directly consider, except in passing, that modern technological progress has drastically lowered the overall level of functioning that we feel is necessary for a normal life. It is very possible that physicians of the distant past might look upon our society of tolerably healthy, reasonably functioning individuals as a world of semi-invalids. Just as we might not be very impressed by the health of an individual who was able to walk through life only if he had a steady diet of tranquilizers or a weekly trip to a dialysis machine. Let us recall that certain long-lived experimental animals often perish rather quickly the moment their artificial supports are removed and they have to fend for themselves in the same environment as their wild cousins.

But by far the most telling point which Dubos makes is one which also leads us back into our question about the relationship between religion and medicine. To say simply that he emphasizes the *social* as well as the vast and interconnected array of physiological factors in the causation of disease may sound like a cliché to most of us who are used to hearing tedious messages about public hygiene and preventative medicine—the very words have long grey beards. But we may begin to take notice as soon as we realize even a few of the factors that make up the structure of the social order. This includes everything a society values, the conception of human relationships, the meaning of the family, the degree of competitiveness which is fostered, the psychological states which are considered tolerable or intolerable (such as boredom, guilt, cheerfulness, grief, emotional expressiveness, and so forth), the relationship to money and material goods, the standards of beauty and proper dress. Of course, these are only a handful of the factors that immediately come to mind. And we must note that we are not speaking here simply about conventionally recognized psychosomatic effects such as ulcers and coronary attacks. But all the factors that enter into the intellectual, emotional, and economic ambience of a society call forth responses from the human body which are mainly unnoticed and habitual. At the same time, these factors and the patterns of living that gather round them lead to contact with chemical and organic substances that enter into the body or that in many other ways have a pronounced effect on the harmonious functioning of the organism.

We have already cited the contact with hydrocarbons and certain atomic radiations as one effect of the modern sense of values and the modern conceptions of nature and our place in it. In the previous century, the social conditions were such as to allow certain microbes their pathogenic influence; thus the diseases which afflict a civilization are bound in an intimate, causal way with the overall patterns of living, which in turn are connected to the ideas and ideals which shape the whole social process in any given era. Therefore, insofar as what we are calling religion is the principal factor in organizing and stabilizing the structure of a civilization, then the practice of medicine can never be independent of religion. The impression one has of the practice of medicine in previous epochs and cultures is that, on the whole, physical healing was never administered without some connection being made to the sense of values, the sense of the meaning and purpose of life, which suffused the culture.

Therefore, the principal concept of disease which all premodern medicine shares (whether Eastern or Western) is that it is the result of a community's failure to live according to the whole truth about the purpose of human life on earth. Traditional, religious language often symbolizes this conception by speaking of a time, long, long ago, when disease did not exist. Thus, according to the Hindu scriptures, bodily disease was unknown in the previous cycles of man's existence on earth. In short, we are speaking here of the idea, expressed repeatedly in the Western Bible, that *disease is a punishment,* an inevitable and lawful result of humankind's failure to live according to its destiny—that is to say, according to its structure and possibilities. It is rather clear, in what we call primitive medicine (for example, among the American Indians) that disease is very often regarded as a phenomenon of society. Thus, the healing methods for certain specific diseases intimately involved the participation of the tribe, which I think anthropologists wrongly interpret and explain solely in terms of the psychological support offered by the tribe to the sick person. There are certain diseases which are understood in terms of the whole community's failure to attend to the higher level in its ways and actions.

The idea of disease as punishment contains much more subtlety than we may think. According to this idea, the human body—like the geocentric earth—is implicated in a vast network of forces and influences, the most important of which can be neither activated nor perceived in man's fallen state of awareness. If there is such a thing as a religion which emanates from a universal level of understanding, such a religion must surely establish the patterns of communal life in full knowledge of the structure of the human organism conceived in this way. Did the founders of the great religious traditions have such knowledge? If so, in what way was it communicated to the masses? That is, are there conceptions about the nature of the human body which require a definite psychological preparation in the same way that certain ideas about the cosmos may require a degree of psychological maturity that is not given to us, but for which we must work?

I cannot claim to know what knowledge about the human body the founders of the great traditions possessed. Nor can I claim to know where, exactly, the line may have been drawn between an inner and an outer system of medicine in traditional societies. It is a fact that the medical texts that have come down to us from ancient times contain a puzzling mixture of recognizably scientific knowledge and what we call magical ideas about spirits, demons, and odd-sounding ritual practices. The medical texts of ancient Egypt and China illustrate this paradox very clearly. For example, the famous Smith Papyrus of Egypt, which is said to date back to 2500 B.C. (though it may have been a copy of a far older document) contains a vast store of anatomical and physiological knowledge that utterly astonished investigators when the first transla-

tions were made. Here are a few abridged lines from the First Instruction
of the Smith Papyrus:

> ... measuring is when you count anything with the *ipt* measure. The
> counting of anything with the fingers (is done) to recognize the way the
> heart goes. There are vessels in it leading to every part of the body. . . .
> When a Sachmet priest . . . puts his fingers to the head . . . to the two
> hands, to the place of the heart . . . to the two legs, then he is measuring
> the heart. . . : it speaks . . . in every vessel, every part of the body . . . one
> measures the vessels of his heart to learn the information that is given by
> it.[10]

The famous Egyptologist, J. H. Breasted, saw this passage as an indication that the ancient Egyptian physicians not only knew about the pulse
as a diagnostic measure, but he also claimed they were on the verge of
discovering the circulation of the blood (which is conventionally
thought to have been unknown until the seventeenth century). We will
probably have to await new breakthroughs in understanding the meaning of ancient Egyptian writings before being able to assess the full range
of medical knowledge they possessed. And such breakthroughs will almost certainly depend not on the talents of the cyptographer, but on a
deeper understanding of the symbolic language in the Egyptian teachings. What we call primitive, magical language may well be symbols of
universal forces expressed in ways that could guide the faculty of intuition in the priest-physician.

2. Medicine and the Two Forces

Because the ancient teachings saw the cosmos as a conscious harmony
of energies, the idea that man is subject to all the forces of creation
served as a call for self-examination to individual men. In Chinese medicine, as in many other ancient systems, disease was understood as the result of interference with this constantly shifting harmony of forces. The
enemy to be feared was not nature, but man's insensitivity to the forces
at work in him. Such a sensitivity by which man could move with the
whole of moving nature is, however, a property of microcosmic man,
perfected man. The hard conclusion is that what the universe cares for
in individual man is only for the perfecting of the microcosm. Great nature is the enemy only of the man who is the enemy of his own perfecting.

The first task of man, therefore, was not to compel nature to make
him comfortable, but to witness in himself more of her laws. No wonder

it is so hard for us to grasp certain ancient medical texts apart from the teaching in which they were originally embedded. Because it was always the external function of a physician to relieve suffering where called upon to do so, we assume that the whole of ancient medical science was geared to this end. But that is not necessarily true, though it is true of our modern system of medical thought. When part of a sacred teaching, medicine is an aspect of the study of how to live in accordance with the laws of inner evolution.

How far this all is from our modern idea of a universe indifferent to life! In such a universe, to be sure, the very existence of life is a miracle and sickness is something to be hated. In a lifeless cosmos, life as we know it has nowhere to go but down. Death is the inevitable end, and suffering of any sort, especially physical suffering, is the herald of death. Time is a "grim reaper."

Staying for a moment with the ancient Chinese system of medicine, we can now see how essential it is to understand why it was based on the metaphysical idea of reality as the meeting and blending of two fundamental energies. Many Westerners are now familiar with the terms *yin* and *yang* and with the sacred diagram by which the teachings of ancient China indicate that every existing thing is the result of the meeting and harmonizing of these two forces. However, the history of modern medicine turns away completely from the effort to understand the relationship of these forces. Just prior to the intellectual triumph of modern scientific medicine, much medical thinking was based on the idea of a natural healing force, a force of life operating in the human body which when left to itself or gently assisted would restore the organism to health. Known as *vitalism*, this concept of a life-force in nature was ultimately rejected as unscientific and sentimental, just as the modern scientific mind rejected the whole Romantic view of nature. Instead, modern science understood the universe as tending toward maximum entropy. The central energy of the universe, therefore, was the energy of death.

Nowadays, we are witnessing a renewed interest in medical systems that emphasize the life-force—homeopathy, naturopathy, so-called folk medicine, and so forth. As part of a general reaction against the scientific world view, it overlaps considerably with the turning toward the religions of Asia. But from the perspective of the Chinese system, both the vitalistic and the mechanistic views of nature are partial and lopsided, being equally expressions of our modern inability to understand energy as the movement between levels, and phenomena as the result of the meeting of vertical forces.

It is surely an error to regard the *yin-yang* of ancient China as representing opposing forces that remain on the same level. To do this is to project our own dualistic thinking onto a form which was, one may be sure, intended to communicate the idea of unity. It must be that the ancient Chinese understood one sort of force as descending from the cosmos to the Earth and the other as *ascending from the Earth toward the cosmos.* If so, then the famous *yin-yang* diagram tells us that *reality, or the Tao, is a blending of an upward and a downward force.*

This is an idea of tremendous magnitude which can show us not only that it was once possible to base the science of medicine on real metaphysics, but also how what we have said about the universe must also be true of human organism—that it is like a teaching which "must be studied like the words of Christ." So, let us go into this idea a little further, setting aside for now the usual associations we bring to the translations of *yin* and *yang* (such as feminine-masculine, darkness-light, active-passive, etc.).

The following expression of the laws of universal forces is from the writings of Chu Hsi, the great sage of twelfth-century China:

> The Supreme Pole [the ultimate principle of the universe] moves and produces the Yang. When the movement has reached its limit, rest ensues. Resting, the Supreme Pole produces the Yin. When the Rest has reached its limit, there is a return to motion. Motion and rest alternate, each being the root of the other. The Yin and Yang take up their appointed functions, and so the Two Forces are established.
>
> The Yang is transformed by reacting with the Yin, and so water, fire, wood, metal and earth are produced. Then these (the Five Elements) diffuse harmoniously, and the Four Seasons proceed on their course.
>
> The Five Elements if combined would form Yin and Yang. Yin and Yang if combined would form the Supreme Pole. . . .
>
> The true principle of that which has no opposite, and the essences of the Two Forces and the Five Elements, react with one another in marvelous ways, and consolidations ensue. The Tao of the heavens perfects maleness and the Tao of the earth perfects femaleness. The Two Elements of maleness and femaleness, reacting with and influencing each other, change and bring the myriad things into being. Generation follows generation and there is no end to their changes and transformations.
>
> It is man alone, however, who receives the finest substance and is the most spiritual of beings. After his bodily form has been produced, his spirit develops consciousness. . . .[11]

Elsewhere in the writings of Chu Hsi, a pupil asks, "Is expansion posi-
tive spiritual force and contraction negative spiritual force?" Chu Hsi
answers by drawing a circle on the desk and pointing to its center:

> Principle is like a circle. Within it there is differentiation like this. All
> cases of material force which is *coming forth* belong to yang and are posi-
> tive spiritual force. All cases of material force which is *returning to its ori-
> gin* belong to yin and are the negative spiritual force.[12]

Recalling that in the language of ancient man, movement downward
equals movement outward, and movement upward equals movement
inward, we have here a universe in process where all things are created,
sustained, and transformed by the harmonization of opposing vertical
forces. There is a force which proceeds outward or downward from the
highest reality and another force, also originating in the highest, which
ultimately resists the downward movement by returning to its source.

As scientists, we say that the universe is indifferent to human need
and we often cite the laws of physics to prove our point. But when New-
ton formulated the laws of motion, he was offering conceptual schemes
that described the universe only as it appears to man in the ordinary
state of consciousness—man, that is, who is not in direct contact with
the higher energies that circulate within himself and the cosmos. And it
is true that ordinary sense-perception presents us with a world that can
be described largely by forces acting laterally, horizontally. From the
ancient perspective, however, the concept of forces acting laterally is an
abstraction, a narrow perception of the whole. The ancient idea that
everything in nature is in movement refers above all to vertical movement and only secondarily, if at all, to lateral movement understood as
perceptible change without change in the quality of being.

It must be added that for ancient man the laws that govern the passage of energies from heaven to earth and back are as inexorable and
impersonal as the laws of physics. It is not that the cosmos is indifferent
to human desire, but that human desire has become, so to say, indifferent to the cosmos.

In any case, the implicit concept of lateral force led scientists of the
last century through the paces of searching for a perpetual motion ma-
chine. When this failed, the notion of increasing entropy was invented,
so that what we were given was a universe which for most practical purposes we could still regard as horizontal, but which for theoretical purposes we must regard as a little bit vertical and downward-directed. The
ancient idea of a life-force had already been flattened out to mean a
force which maintains an organism instead of a force which constantly

transforms all entities by either the process of disintegration (death) or the process of perfection (life), both processes being necessary to each other and, as it were, one feeding off the other. Naturally, the modern, flattened version of the idea of a life-force seemed sentimental, being the metaphysical projection of a psychological fear.

Thus, the ancient Chinese system of medicine understands the healthy human being as a little universe containing and harmonizing the entire reach of the two fundamental processes of the great universe. For man, therefore, the life-force cannot operate automatically but requires that he bring into harmony all the energies at his disposal, including of course the energies which lie at the source of what is named intellect, will, conscience, and consciousness. This is the metaphysical basis of the idea, expressed in varying ways in various traditions, that disease is a punishment from God. This punishment has nothing at all to do with our literal understanding of the word. It refers mainly to the inevitable results of man's unwillingness or inability to attend to all the energies within him.

Nor does it mean that all disease must be countered by direct efforts of the will, as has often been claimed. It is extraordinary how much stupidity we have attributed to men whose psychological and moral teachings we acknowledge to spring from a nearly miraculous source of wisdom. An exceptionally important matter is at stake here concerning the complexity of man and the nature of his relationship to that complexity, and concerning above all the transcendent spiritual function called common sense. In the great teachings, man is many things. There *are* functions in him that are relatively automatic; he *is* in certain aspects a mere animal; and therefore there are diseases (and much else) which do not require him to think, feel, or act in extraordinary ways. Sometimes, he needs ordinary help from ordinary men; sometimes he needs miraculous help from miraculous sources. Some diseases are, as it has been called, natural in their causation; others, in the words of Paracelsus, whom we have already cited, are "sent by God as a punishment, as a warning, as a sign by which we know that all our affairs are naught, that our knowledge rests on no firm foundation, and that the truth is not known to us, but that we are inadequate and fragmentary in all ways, and that no ability or knowledge is ours."

But what is required of man is something in its way far more extraordinary than the supernatural functions which many teachings tell us are latent in him. Man is required to *discriminate*, to "know each thing's name," words echoing the Book of Genesis and applying, surely, to the processes or creatures within a man as well as to the creatures of external nature.

In my opinion, it is this ability to discriminate the metaphysical quality of various organic processes (including diseases) that really sets ancient medicine apart from the modern. Modern physicians are very often refreshingly flexible and eclectic. Apart from its marked drawbacks as a guide for thinking about reality, the contemporary pragmatic criterion has given us a certain maneuverability at least in medical practice. But from the point of view of ancient systems such as the Chinese, modern medicine is *not eclectic enough,* in a sense. Man is more things than we imagine; more processes take place in him than we know. So, taking into account all the various forms of medicine that are now being practiced in addition to the orthodox—homeopathy, faith-healing, herbalism, natureopathy, chiropractic, etc.—it is not really a question of settling on one that corresponds to the ancient understanding of the human organism, but of finding in ourselves a quality of attention and discrimination that is one of the central attributes of what is called a higher state of consciousness.

As has already been noted, historians of medicine are often perplexed by what they see as an incomprehensible mixture of rational medical practice and magic in ancient civilizations. But if there did once exist a sacred science of medicine, if medicine was once an aspect and an expression of genuine psychospiritual discipline, it should not be surprising that physicians existed who were able to exercise this power of discriminating among qualities of energy in the human organism. Could it be that what we label magic was, in some cases and among some peoples, a means of relating to certain energies which we today are no longer able to perceive, much less master? Is the fear which drives us to try to be conquerors of nature a factor which has reduced our sensitivity to these energies? And are we mentally comfortable only when dealing with what we consider destructive forces—forces that from a larger perspective represent only a narrow band of the spectrum of downward and upward energies?

The subject of magic and medicine can therefore provide us with much food for thought. We hear about primitive medicine men driving out evil spirits. But what, exactly, are these spirits? Are they only the constructs of a superstitious imagination? Perhaps, often, they are. But perhaps they are a reference to certain energies of which we are unaware, for reasons we have already discussed. It is certainly no help to bring in the concept of *suggestion* in order to account for the apparent efficacy of these magical practices. And it is no help because this concept of suggestion is based on psychological theories which themselves are products of modern medical-scientific thinking which, as we have said, only acknowledges the existence of a very narrow range of universal forces. It is moreover an absurd presumption to assume that archaic man or the precolonial American Indian suffered from just the sort of neurotic conflict that characterizes contemporary civilizations.

To introduce ourselves more intelligently to the subject of sacred medicine, let us look at the Navajo tradition. What is the function of the famous Navajo sandpaintings, which irresistibly call to mind the sacred diagrams or mandalas of the Tibetan tradition? What psycho-physical preparation does the Navajo way of life provide such that the making and contemplation of these cosmic diagrams, and even the act of sitting inside them, connects the Navajo to forces that have obvious physical effects? Is the continuous chanting, which to our ears may sound like mumbo-jumbo, based on the same understanding of sound-vibration that one finds in every other spiritual discipline that we know, including of course the mantra-yoga of Asia? And what are we to make of the reports by the pioneering American researcher, Washington Matthews, that novices learning this ceremonial are sometimes physically injured by the energies which it released, and that he himself suffered a paralytic stroke while learning it?[13]

Then there is the dancing. Is it only a means of what we moderns call religious expression, or can specific postures and movements—together with certain precisely controlled bodily efforts—"make straight the paths of the Lord," that is, evoke in the dancer the flow of a more conscious force that can be perceived even by a spectator?

On the subject of effort, how are we to understand that disease is often treated by demanding of the patient a degree of physical activity that strikes us as naïve, or even dangerous? (For example, the Koniaga medicine man wrestles his patient in order to drive out the spirit; in other tribes the patient is required to sit cross-legged, without ever lying down to sleep, for many days at a time.)

It is worth noting that the Cheyenne understood the word "medicine" to mean energy, and Vogel claims in his monumental study of American Indian medicine, that the term applies to a whole array of ideas and concepts, as well as to remedies and treatments.[14]

In short, it is possible that we put the label "magic" on methods and phenomena we simply do not understand, where causal relationships exist we do not acknowledge—just as any child or primitive man might regard the results of our own technology. Therefore, the whole question of verifying for ourselves the value of certain ancient medical practices revolves around the development of a finer inward sensitivity to energy, and has little to do with the outward duplication of techniques. The point is that without this sensitivity the remedies may not work, for sensitivity to finer energies is not understood only as a bare witnessing, but as that which effects the channelling process by which these energies in fact pass from one place (in ourselves) to another.

In a strange way, therefore, our modern fear of nature is justified—but only so long as we remain cut off from the full scale of cosmic energies which is the birthright of microcosmic man. There is nothing mysterious or dark about this thought. An acorn which falls not on soil but on rock has just as much reason to be afraid of nature. It too is, so to say, cut off—for itself—from the full scale of ascending and descending forces which are possible for it. And, while it is still used by nature for nature's purposes (an animal eats it), it will never become an oak tree.

Is our contemporary civilization such that we modern men are like acorns which have fallen on rock? And what is the craft of medicine for such an acorn? To put the first question is to ask how we modern men have become alienated from the cosmos. And the latter question, while helping us to see that present-day medicine is but another expression of the modern psyche, will also reveal why it is in the long run futile to attack today's medical theories apart from the question of man's disturbed inner connection to universal forces.

3. The Two Sciences

The point at issue is whether the human body can be studied in order to bring us self-knowledge and an understanding of our place in the universal order, as well as in order to hold back death and physical suffering. Surely, this is the only intelligent way to understand the possibility of medicine as a sacred science.

The elusiveness of a sacred study of the body is well illustrated by one of the most brilliant physiological essays of the twentieth century. In 1932 Dr. Walter Cannon brought together a tremendous amount of physiological data under the concept of *homeostasis,* the extraordinarily complex chemical equilibrium which the body must maintain throughout its life.[15]

> When we consider the extreme instability of our bodily structure, its readiness for disturbance by the slightest application of external forces and the rapid onset of its decomposition as soon as favoring circumstances are withdrawn, its persistence through many decades seems almost miraculous. The wonder increases when we realize that the system is open, engaging in free exchange with the outer world. . . .[16]

Soon after, he cites the dictum of the famous French physiologist, Claude Bernard, to the effect that "all the vital mechanisms, however varied they may be, have only one object, that of preserving constant the conditions of life in the internal environment."[17] Cannon's entire book is a demonstration of this dictum as it applies to the regulation of body temperature, oxygen supply, the chemical balance of the blood, and so forth. To this day, the notion of *homeostasis* remains a cornerstone of scientific thought about bodily processes, and every textbook of physiology bears its imprint.

Reading this book, one gradually begins to feel a sort of schizophrenia setting in. One marvels at the facts which Cannon's thesis allows him to bring forth and yet the thesis itself is, so to say, less intelligent than the processes it embraces. The purposes of this whole organism and all its processes is simply to stay in one place until the inevitable defeat of death. One is left with the impression that the sole aim of life is to evolve more and more complex and futile ways of excluding death. Nature itself is made to seem schizophrenic through this emphasis on *lateral homeostasis,* an equilibrium of lateral energies.

The impression that science projects our fear of nature upon its perceptions of the organism is particularly marked where Dr. Cannon discusses "the margin of safety" in bodily structure and functions. How are our bodies built? He asks, "Are they set up with niggardly economy? Is barely enough provision made for keeping us intact? Or is there allowance for contingencies—have safety factors been introduced on which we may count in times of stress?"

His answer, of course, is that the body is built with an incredibly wide "safety margin." A man may live quite normally, for example, with only one kidney—indeed, two-thirds of each kidney may be taken without serious disturbance. One-tenth of adrenal tissue is all that is really necessary for the body, and four-fifths of thyroid substance may be removed without abnormal effects. Only one-fifth of the pancreas is needed to furnish the insulin which the organism requires, and as for the busiest and most versatile organ of the body, the liver, three-fourths of it may be lost without serious harm. Ten feet of the small intestine (normally twenty-three feet long) was removed from one patient and in many cases almost all of the large intestine was cleared away with results that actually seem to have been beneficial. Cannon cites many other examples: blood sugar and calcium levels, systolic pressure, lung capacity, are all greater than need be. Even great areas of the brain are expendable, according to Cannon. He reports of one patient who, after surgical removal of both frontal lobes, "was perfectly aware of time, place, and person; the memory was unimpaired; he read, wrote, and passed mathematical tests accurately, and in conversation was not distinguishable from a normal individual." Recent advances in brain research and neurosurgery have added even more data to Cannon's picture.

But what exactly is this picture? Are we quite sure that we see it all in the only way possible? Imagine that I have stepped inside a huge, complex factory; everywhere there are enormous and intricate machines merely idling. My companion guesses that this is the safety factor for times of stress when there is a great demand for production, as most of the time the work of the factory takes place in one small building. Perhaps this is so, but the thought crosses my mind that since this factory was designed for much more work than is being asked of it, perhaps the owner, who has only just inherited it, does not really understand all the work for which these machines are designed. Perhaps he has grown so content with its limited production, and so afraid of being deprived of it, that he cannot see it any other way.

This metaphor provides one obvious clue concerning the difficulty of a sacred study of the body. No amount of speculation or authoritative advice will persuade the owner of this factory to use it differently so long as his fear has the upper hand. We may read as many ancient texts as we please concerning the meaning of the various organs of the body, but as long as the fear of pain and death is uppermost in our minds we will remain pragmatic. We will not be free to look at this body impartially, as one may read a book. The conquest of fear is therefore the main prerequisite for learning about ourselves through a study of the body.

This must certainly be one reason why ancient man joined medicine with religious discipline. It cannot lead one far to study the body without at the same time directly studying one's own thoughts and emotions, as was done in the great psycho-spiritual disciplines. This same problem exists with respect to understanding a sacred book. When we turn to scripture directly, without having attempted to see the whole of ourselves in our relationship to life, the result is a too literal understanding. We read the text in the light of habitual mental associations which serve our fears and desires, and consequently our reading of the sacred book only strengthens what needs to be weakened, and only weakens what needs to be strengthened. Thus it is said that all great teaching is *indirect*.

May we not suggest, then, that to heal the sick and to promote physical health is the outer or exoteric side of the science of medicine, while to study the body in order to understand the cosmic laws is its inner or sacred dimension? Looking at medicine in this way, we are immediately rid of certain confusions surrounding the renewed modern interest in systems of medicine that seem to echo ancient times. The adherents of these nonorthodox systems claim that their methods work better. Perhaps often they do. Perhaps in many areas homeopathy, say, or chiropractic are more effective than modern orthodox treatments. But from the point of view we are exploring, all modern medicine—orthodox and nonorthodox—falls under the same umbrella: they study the body in order to *preserve* the body. Sacred medicine, on the other hand, adds to this the intention of studying the body in order to *transcend* the body. It is obvious, then, that modern man does not wish for a sacred science of medicine, no matter what great and ancient ideas he infuses into his medical theories.

Did there once exist a craft of medicine which alleviated suffering without thickening the veil between man and death? Certain aspects of ancient texts suggest that possibility. We have already mentioned that among the ancient Egyptian writings, for example, one finds both a sophisticated knowledge of pharmacology and surgery and an extensive, bewildering application of *magic*. The same is true of ancient China, the American Indian, and almost every traditional civilization of which we have sufficient record. It seems that the traditional mind recognizes two sorts of disease just as it recognizes two sorts of suffering: one it is incumbent upon man to expel and the other it is incumbent upon man to take in: one profane and the other sacred.

In general, modern man is displeased by the distinction between educative or redemptive suffering and suffering that is unnecessary or evil. This is a subject which would require an extensive examination of the modern science of psychology. Here we need only mark in our thought the distinction between purgation and waste, between a process that separates higher from lower and one that mixes and confuses them. We shall find our way back to the idea of disease as punishment only when we begin to understand that the psycho-spiritual meaning of punishment is purgation. And we shall connect the craft of medicine to sacred teachings only if we remember that the goal of such teachings is to awaken in man a relationship to the greater energies of consciousness, and that for this to take place a man must be purged of his false sense of agency.

I find this a very helpful way of looking at traditional man's blending of religion and medicine. Like everyone else, I had always assumed that ritualistic medicine was mainly superstition and primitive psychotherapy. Absurdly underestimating the function of religion, we naturally misunderstand the historical association of religion and medicine. But now we begin to see that what we take to be ancient man's naïve efforts to preserve the physical body were often his rather extraordinary methods of creating a confrontation in the body between divine energies and the physiological results of egoism. The goal of such a confrontation would surely have been both the restoration of health and the preparation for death. That these two go hand in hand is something we find incomprehensible. But I believe it is almost the definition of sacred medicine: *the simultaneous restoration of health and preparation for death.*

What must give us pause in all of this is the idea that a conscious universe does not exist for the ego, the isolated intellect, the self that I am when I imagine I am a self. That is to say, what surely must give us pause is the idea which ancient traditions communicate across the years that I may be diseased because I am no longer in relationship to the greater forces passing through me. And that I then become a puppet of these same forces as they act outside me on the great scale of nature and the universe, affecting the masses of humanity and organic life—in which I and my body are but a speck.

In such a state of consciousness, the laws of death, the scale of death, threatens man as an enemy threatens. Against it he is utterly powerless. The great crime of modern science is only that with it we persevere in believing that the real world is the world that appears to the ego with its isolated intellect and its fears that breed pragmatism. No wonder we have transformed medicine into a system for the temporary preservation of the ego.

The idea of sacred medicine teaches us that the universe is conscious only to conscious man, and that there are states of being in which universally active forces can reach my body from within my body. These forces cannot act upon my body from without, except as my body is part of organic life on earth with its great cycles of life, death, fertilization, and decay. The ego cannot battle against that either in nature or in the body. Man in the state of egoism is crushed by the universe, both actually and in theory. The ego alone with all its bodily habits to support it lives in a hostile universe because it constantly fights to preserve itself. It is a euphemism to speak of the universe of modern science as unalive, nonliving. We call it a dead universe because we are unable to bear that our state of consciousness evokes a hostile universe. Traditional man was clearer about the enmity we gather when we live severed from a higher consciousness. It is a lawful enmity to be sure, not directed to me personally, but it is a genuine enmity and to communicate this it is not so far from the mark to speak of evil spirits and of *punishment*.

Thinking such thoughts, how can we ever again look with condescension upon the rituals of so-called primitive medicine. We naïvely believe these rituals had only a psychological effect and we hastily compare them to our more sophisticated methods of psychosomatic medicine. But psychosomatic medicine seeks to preserve the ego; sacred medicine sought to free man from self-illusion and its physiological consequences. The one manipulates our habits of feeling so as to reestablish the habits of the body while of the other we can only surmise that it offered man the chance to understand upon what in the universe his well-being really depended.

REFERENCES

1. Paracelsus, *Selected Writings,* ed. Jolande Jacobi, Bollingen Series XXVIII, 2nd ed. (Princeton: Princeton University Press, 1969), pp. 63–68.
2. *Ibid.,* p. 81.
3. Charles Singer and E. Ashworth Underwood, *A Short History of Medicine* (London and New York: Oxford University Press, 1962), p. 92.
4. Benjamin Lee Gordon, *Medieval and Renaissance Medicine* (New York: Philosophical Library, 1959), pp. 1–2.
5. See L. Edelstein, *Ancient Medicine* (Baltimore: Johns Hopkins University Press, 1967).
6. Heinrich R. Zimmer, *Hindu Medicine* (Baltimore: Johns Hopkins University Press, 1948), pp. 75–76.
7. *Ibid.,* pp. 63–73.
8. René Dubos, *Mirage of Health* (New York: Doubleday, Anchor Books, 1961), p. 30.
9. *Ibid.,* p. 170.
10. Quoted in Juergen Thorwald, *Science and Secrets of Early Medicine* (Harlow, Essex, England: Longmans, Green, 1962).
11. Adapted from Joseph Needham, *Science and Civilization in China,* vol. 2 (London and New York: Cambridge University Press, 1962), pp. 460–642.
12. Wing-Tsit Chang, *A Source Book in Chinese Philosophy* (Princeton: Princeton University Press, 1963), p. 644.
13. Frank Waters, *Masked Gods* (Denver: Sage Books, 1950), pp. 256–257: "And of late years Reichard, in her two-volume study of *Navajo Religion* records that the singer, Crawler, incurred paralysis of the legs (and his name) because he was too weak to stand the power of this same great chant."
14. Virgil J. Vogel, *American Indian Medicine* (Norman: University of Oklahoma Press, 1970), pp. 24–25.
15. Walter B. Cannon, *Wisdom of the Body* (1932; reprint ed., New York: W. W. Norton, 1963).
16. *Ibid.,* p. 20.
17. *Ibid.,* p. 38.

MAGIC, SACRIFICE, AND TRADITION: PRELIMINARY NOTES

As a professor in the field of comparative religion, I have had frequent occasion to study the practices of magic in ancient traditions, such as existed in Pharaonic Egypt, in Tibet, among the Kabalistic Jews. . . .

No, I had better not finish that sentence. It is true that I have read books about these traditions, and many other traditions which contain rituals that we group under the label of magic. And I have studied some of the sacred texts of these teachings, their symbols, their metaphysics and cosmology. But what does that mean—to have studied a tradition? And how have I—how do we—in fact read their sacred books? In these questions there is contained a serious difficulty which needs to be exposed.

I recall the words of a scholar I once knew in my college days, a renowned authority on the traditions and culture of ancient China. He had published dozens of important studies and had received every award and accolade which the academic world had to offer a man in his field. He was regularly consulted by governments, mapmakers, linguists and, in his later years—to his great surprise—by young people searching not only for academic guidance, but for spiritual advice. I happened to have a temporary part-time job delivering and collecting library books and had a number of *en passant* conversations with him in his office.

Every inch of his incredibly disorganized room was piled to the ceiling with stacks of books and papers which I indifferently pushed around when performing my job as delivery boy. One day I accidentally knocked over a large stack of Chinese texts, several of which fell open in front of me. My attention was caught by some illustrations of the human body drawn in a very peculiar way with strange symbols surrounding it in concentric circles. Being on rather informal terms with this great scholar, before whom everyone else bowed and scraped, I was able to say something like, "What in God's name are these?"

He looked up from his tiny, dimly lit desk and craned his old neck to see what had captured me.

"That is a text of Taoist incantations," he said flatly. "That particular diagram was used to kill enemies from a distance merely through the pronouncement of certain syllables."

In those days I had a pretty cold eye toward anything that wasn't gilded with modern, scientific credentials. I shook my head and squatted over the text to look at it more carefully. Suddenly I began to feel an odd vibration in my abdomen. My scientific mind flew right out the window.

After a few minutes, he looked up from his papers again, surprised to see me still peering wide-eyed at the strange diagram. He suddenly gave out a rather loud sound of disgust which startled me so much that I fell back into a sitting posture.

"Needleman, shut that book!"

I did so.

Then he pushed away the papers that were in front of him and swiveled back in his chair, waving his hand at the hundreds of books on the walls and floor.

"Needleman, do you know what journalism is?"

"Certainly," I said, though I immediately realized that he was giving the word a special meaning.

"There are three, maybe four books in this whole room that are not journalism. But all the rest, including that one on the floor, are journalism. Even the books I have written myself are just that, journalism."

He cupped his hands together on his lap and became quite still in his chair. I stayed where I was.

"Needleman, I am practically at the end of my life. I know more about Chinese religion than maybe anyone in the world, maybe even more than the Chinese themselves. Yet the most important thing I don't know. Because I have never felt the tradition. And therefore I have never understood the real arrangement of the elements of the tradition.

"I have only just begun to realize this. In order to *know* what one knows, one must feel."

At that moment a student knocking at the door interrupted him and he never spoke to me again in that way. For some reason I did not have the interest or the courage to ask him what he meant, what kind of feeling he was talking about. For he was certainly not advocating emotionalism, or sentimentality, or the destruction of the canons of objectivity. The only thing he ever said that seemed to relate to that conversation was one half-mumbled statement some months later to the effect that "tradition originates in a very high place."

All this comes back to me quite strongly now because of the extreme difficulty of saying one honest word about magic. The difficulty lies in the struggle to be sufficiently open to everything that one has heard, read, and dreamed about magic. Why has it often been condemned by the orthodoxy, even while forming an integral part of the rites and rituals in many traditions? And why this tendency in modern thought to treat magic as though it existed apart from the forms of tradition?

For there lies the real power—the dark power if you wish—of the figure of the magician. He stands outside the sanctioned rules and the forms; he emerges out of the shadows in contact with a force that is strangely, perhaps dangerously, greater than anything human, greater than anything in creation save the power of God.

Touched, drawn, burned by this symbol, we begin to think of magic as the exercise of powers that have nothing to do with the central crisis of the human situation—the darkness of illusion about ourselves and the destruction within us of the energy of life. We begin to link the symbolism of magic with fragmentary psychic phenomena such as telepathy or clairvoyance.

Such phenomena are indeed inexplicable by present scientific assumptions. I myself have witnessed them several times, but under conditions which made it irrelevant and impossible to reach for explanations. But in the present general conditions of intellectual life, such things when they genuinely happen merely agitate our minds. When something inexplicable happens either outside or inside of us the new quality of attention that is generated cannot withstand our urge to build theories. In the process we hardly notice that we have lost a certain attentiveness to ourselves, a certain sensitivity of feeling that is the seed of an impartial mind.

Let us make a distinction, therefore, between magic considered as isolated, inexplicable phenomena, and magic that is part of a spiritual tradition or, at the very least, that is defined and recognized by one or another spiritual tradition.

In making this distinction, in limiting magic to its connection with spiritual tradition, we accomplish at least one thing: we make the question of magic something *serious*. We take it out of the realm of a symbol understood so literally that it degenerates into wishful thinking. Spiritual tradition is serious—at least as serious as, for example, the problem of personal unhappiness, a broken leg, a child's death, a scornful look from my neighbor. And then our question becomes, what does the fact of magic mean in terms of ourselves as we really are—beings swept away by the emotions of everyday life, even as our minds soar out of contact with our true internal situation?

The fact that, from the point of view of tradition, magic is hidden or dangerous now begins to speak to us in a new way: The miraculous cannot appear and must not be sought without first facing ourselves as what we are. There are extraordinary, miraculous possibilities in human life, but they cannot appear in place of the ordinary possibilities. And the first message of tradition is that as we actually are we are not even ordinary men.

But what does that mean: we are not even ordinary men? Is it our failure to understand this idea that prevents us from *feeling* the purpose of tradition and which therefore makes all our perceptions and theories about religion and magic merely journalism? Take it even more directly: Is it our failure to *feel* the contradictions of the human condition, our own human condition, that bars us from genuinely experiencing the magical possibilities of life?

This idea has been forcefully expressed in the novel, *Strange Life of Ivan Osokin*, by P. D. Ouspensky.

Ivan Osokin is a young man who has watched himself stupidly take the wrong turn at every crossroads of his life until he is brought to the state of desperation. At the point of suicide, he visits a powerful old magician. In the course of talking to the magician, Osokin pleads for a chance to live his life over again, knowing in advance everything that has happened before. "It is possible," the magician says, "but it will not make things better for you . . . I can send you back as far as you like, and you will remember everything, but nothing will come of it."

Not believing the magician, Osokin asks to be transported back to his school days. But his life proceeds as the magician predicted. Osokin knows what will happen, but he cannot bring that knowledge into his emotional life, and inexorably everything takes place exactly as before, down to the last detail, until he even ignores what he knows and imagines it to be only a dream. In short, he is trapped again in the wheel of existence.

Once more he is brought to the point of despair, and once more he finds himself in the magician's house. But now one thing is different: Osokin realizes with horror what has happened. He knows and *feels* the automatism of ordinary human life. "There is the cold of the grave in this thought. He feels that this is the fear of the inevitable, fear of himself, of that self from which there is no escape. . . . He will be the same and everything will be the same."

Then, and only then, does he find it in himself to sacrifice his belief that he knows what he needs and ask for help without dictating the terms. And only then can the magician show him the first step toward the path of escape from the innate automatism of his existence. He tells Osokin:

". . . Nothing can be acquired without sacrifice. This is the thing you do not understand, and until you understand it, nothing can be done. Had I wanted to give you, without any sacrifice on your part, everything you might wish, I could not have done it.

"A man can be given only what he can use; and he can use only that for which he has sacrificed something. This is the law of human nature. So if a man wants to get help to acquire important knowledge or new powers, he must sacrifice other things important to him at the moment. Moreover, he can only get as much as he has given up for it. . . ."

"Are there no other ways?" asks Osokin.

The magician answers, "You mean ways in which no sacrifices are necessary? No, there are no such ways, and you do not understand what you are asking. You cannot have results without causes. By your sacrifice you create causes. . . ."

Can we hear the voice of tradition, as well as a far more serious understanding of magic, in these words?

If we cannot, I suggest that it is because something has gone very wrong in our understanding of religion, not to mention the aspects of both religion and magic, such as the act of sacrifice and its inner significance.

I should like to explain what I mean as faithfully as possible, for in my opinion we are now at the edge of an idea that throws a clear light not only on the nature of magic, but on the specific difficulties of the modern spiritual search. The idea is not my own invention, but when I first heard of it—which was quite recently—it struck me as being so central that I could not believe it had escaped me all these years. Suddenly, everything I had ever known about the relationship between magic and religion seemed almost childish in comparison—or, at the very least, so subjective that no genuine search could be supported by it. I will present it the way it was told to me by an elderly Christian monk whom I came to know at a conference which I recently attended in the Far East.

This particular monk, by the way, never told me the name of his Order, only that it was located in the Middle East and had existed for many centuries. My own surmise was that he was not part of what is officially recognized as the Christian Church, but was instead a member of a still surviving Gnostic sect. However that may be, we had several private conversations in the course of which he said many extraordinary things about the ancient origins of the Christian tradition. I will relate these claims and try to evaluate them in a forthcoming book dealing with the contemporary search for the original Christian tradition.*

The pertinent material here, however, concerns what he said in response to a theory I put forth to him about the office of the priest-magician in the religious systems of archaic man. I based my theory on ideas which I had arrived at while writing about magic in my book *A Sense of the Cosmos*. It seemed to me that the study of illusion, due to the undeveloped power of attention in "fallen man," must have been an essential element in the ancient traditions. By "illusion" I meant not only perceptual illusion, which the trickster can effect, but the deeper illusions about ourselves and our world, under which we suffer as a result of mankind's deep-seated slavery to self-suggestibility. Before I had a chance to develop my thoughts further, he interrupted me (he spoke in rather broken English, which I will not attempt to duplicate here):

"Yes, that is very true as far as it goes. But it is not the main point, or rather, it is only part of the main point. What people in the modern world do not know is that religion is something which actually works, which produces tangible changes at the deepest levels of the human organism. In all these conferences and meetings that I have been attending I have seen that even Eastern peoples are forgetting that real religion is based on precise laws of nature which, when applied correctly, produce extraordinary results that are called miraculous only because people do not understand these laws.

"Because modern religion does not produce real results, the whole question of magic is irrelevant. But in ancient times, and among authentic traditions which still survive, the interdependence between religion and magic is so crucial that without a proper understanding of this interdependence it is absolutely impossible for man to attain to his real spiritual birthright.

"I shall put it very simply so that we do not get lost in details concerning rituals and various symbolic expressions, nor indulge ourselves criticizing what happens when these rituals become cut off from the genuine wellspring of the tradition. To put it in one word: *Religion* is the part of a tradition which shows man his helplessness apart from God; *Magic* is the part of tradition which brings about tangible results that are lawfully caused by the painful and precisely guided sacrifice of spiritual illusions.

"Religion empties a man; magic fills him with the power to act from

---

* Jacob Needleman, *Lost Christianity* (New York: Doubleday & Co., 1980).

the vital center of himself as a being made in the image of his creator.

"As I have said, all real religion produces results, but the question of how to be toward these results is the most difficult and easily lost element in a teaching. It is the very first thing to go when a tradition begins to degenerate. But both magic and religion are necessary components of every complete tradition.

"Without magic, religion turns man against nature, the creation of God, and eventually against God himself.

"Without magic, religion abandons the inner sensations that support the forces of hope and love. Religious man may know he is nothing under God, but without magic he no longer spontaneously feels the goodness and warmth of this hard truth, no longer seeks to apply it to *himself* out of the instincts of the heart. Instead, he applies this truth to his neighbor's weaknesses, and eventually he may even kill his neighbor. Without magic, man loses the sense of wonder before the creation that is within himself, the transformation and destruction of forms within the psyche, the constant liberation and movement of his own inner energies. Only such self-knowledge can generate real pity for my own neighbor and also real knowledge of him and a true sense of justice toward him.

"Man must have results, real results, in his inner and outer life. I do not mean the results which modern people strive after. These are not results, but only rearrangements of psychic material, a process which the Asian peoples call *samsara* and which our Holy Bible calls 'dust.'

"Without religion, however, magic by itself draws man fatally under the thrall of disincarnate beings who pervade the earth and feed upon the emotional energies of the human organism. These are called demons, but the word has ceased to have anything but a childish meaning for modern people. I shall try to use contemporary language for you, but you must remember that contemporary language is not based on actual experience of such forces.

"What we call the world is the creation of mind descending into form and substance. For a moment, set aside all your familiar associations with philosophical theories of the past or present. This is not philosophy.

"Have you ever seen a scientific illustration of a nerve entering a muscle in the human body? That is an exact analogy of what I am speaking about. The nerve transmits a psychic energy which is transformed by the muscle into mechanical energy. We see the external movements of living beings for what they are—patterns of material mechanism. What we do not see is that a law of descent is at work, from the psychic to the material. That is what is called biological life.

"In the human animal, as well as in all higher animate life, the fundamental psychic energy which is transmitted to the muscles is twofold: instinctual and emotional. The transmission of instinctual psychic energy into matter takes place on a very general scale through the species-structure of all living beings. It cannot vary in individual animals of the same species. But the emotional psychic energy is different; it is the central power of all relatively individuated higher animals, those whom Buddhists of certain lineages call 'sentient beings.'

"There are many factors I am not mentioning, and other gradations of energy between the mechanical and the psychic. But the point I am making is that the world of life is to a great extent created and maintained through the expression of emotional energy. And it is this energy through which magic operates. Results, the results which I am speaking to you about, are always the products of a certain quality of emotion.

"Modern man believes he has created his world through intellect and action. But it is not true. He is fallen man and his intellect is the servant of emotion, just as are his voluntary muscles.

"What you call primitive man looks at the modern technological world and sees a form of magic. You laugh at him, but he is right. The modern, nontraditional world has come into being through emotional energy that is formed into the pattern called egoism, with its aspects of fear, desire, and self-protectiveness. I will not say anything more about the larger forces which this modern process is serving because you would think I am indulging in what is called occultism.

"The control and manipulation of emotional energy is the secret of all magic, black or white. The black magician agitates the mind until a certain intensity of emotional force is evoked in people. From that point, depending on his skill, he can make them do or see whatever he wishes, for in the state of mental agitation the controlling power of human attention—which is the specific energy that distinguishes man from the animal—is totally absorbed by each passing thought-association and the passion to act that accompanies it; in such a state man is even more the prey of suggestion than normally. And an external manipulator, concentrating on a specific aim, can control the mind and subjectively perceived reality of another human being. However, in the ordinary conditions of modern life, external suggestions do not often follow one straight line. There is only a criss-cross of suggestions coming from countless ever-new sources.

"Tradition does not work with either mechanical or psychic energy, but with a different level of force which one could call spiritual energy. This manifests in man in the form of an extraordinary quality of emotion and, in rare cases, of an intellectual power which is completely unknown to the rest of us.

"To awaken spiritual emotion is the work of religious discipline. And this comes about through the sacrifice of attachment to results—*even as they are taking place in a man.* Religious man may become a powerful magician but through it he sees only the greatness of God and the nullity of his own being. The energies of egoistic emotion that are bound to his inner results are immediately separated from these results and are transformed upward, or rather are connected to the energy that created the world itself."

To these words I can now add nothing but the determination to ponder their meaning.

THE ART OF LIVING IN THE CULTURAL REVOLUTION

HOW to live? Is it any wonder that this most ancient of questions has resurfaced? You say, "But it has always existed, this question." Not so; other questions once took its place, especially in the recent history of mankind: how to serve God? how to be happy? how to know nature? how to help others? how to be safe? We need to be clear about this: the question of how to live directs us to start completely from zero in our approach to life.

It was Plato's question two and a half millennia ago. The gods of Greece were dead and the sciences of the physical world had lost their luster. Socrates walked the streets of Athens in a time not unlike our own when, as it has been observed, only lesser thinkers invested much hope in the process of physical discovery. Socrates taught men to begin from zero, giving themselves wholly neither to the world of the gods nor to the world of the senses, neither to the inner world nor to the outer.

Philosophy in the Western world was born as the art and science of beginning from nothing, from pure self-inquiry. Through this, men were called to attend to the world *between* the gods and the senses, the world of the self, *my*self. Who among the pupils of Socrates answered this call in the spirit in which it was sounded? Plato? Perhaps—perhaps not. But in any case the most profound written response produced by Plato was *The Republic*. There the figure of Socrates is made to answer the question of how to live by setting aside the whole structure of culture and civilization as it was known, and building the new society from zero—the new man from zero. Through the work of self-inquiry both the inner world of the mind and the outer world of nature are brought into contact and relationship. Whether or not the living message of Socrates was lost even as early as Plato, we can see that neither the religion nor science of his day had the power to withstand the force of the Socratic interrogation.

Now, approaching the end of the twentieth century, Western man finds himself once again suspended between the gods of the world of the senses. The names of course are different and the appearances are different. But as in the time of Socrates serious people find they can no longer move with integrity toward either realm, while at the same time the pull of each increases with every passing day. The world of religion has returned from eclipse—now as a new mysticism, a call to interiority. Fragments of spiritual traditions from the East, and from the sacred teachings of the West as well, call out to us, offering the ancient way of transcendence. Yet more rapidly than ever before the influence of science increases, transforming every aspect of our lives, every single detail of living. The world of the senses now exists in the form of the new technologies with all their promise and peril. The role of these new technologies in our life is overwhelming; they cannot be ignored, no more than our ancestors could ignore the forces of nature. Technology has become more than a way of dealing with nature; it is now, in its own right, a major force in the life of humanity on this planet. And like nature itself, it has many faces, both awesome and beautiful, terrifying and alluring.

It is necessary to emphasize how different the place of science is at the present moment. It has become something *new* in our life, quite different from its role even a generation ago. Utopian thinkers of the industrial revolution who presented images of man's new tenure on earth were not grappling with the same question of how to live that is before us now. The new world drawn by the artists and philosophers of the early modern era was a world of hope, in which the ancient values of religion were now to be actualized through the new dispensation of science and reason. This vision, as we can see now, was an outward thrust, a movement toward the manipulation of nature.

Contemporary man, however, exists in a world already extensively manipulated by scientific technology. It is no longer predominantly man confronting nature, but man confronting the results of technology. The problem of how to live meets us here at the point of contact between ourselves and the world shaped by science. Ultimately, of course, nature still holds sway—in the inescapable laws of birth and death. But increasingly rarely do we consciously meet the raw forces of nature. Our problem is how to live among the methods we have developed for meeting nature.

To sense the dimensions of our problem, it is enough to ask what has become of the perennial moral values of Western man. Certainly, they still remain as ideals. But we are asking, what does it mean to live them in the contemporary milieu? Even as ideals, they are shaky. The established religions of the West, in long retreat against the onslaught of scientism; the philosophical minds of the past three centuries, allying themselves with the sensory-based canons of scientific knowledge: both these forces of Western thought have ceased to assure the symbolic and metaphysical foundations of the perennial morality of mankind.

But focusing our attention on the practical question of living according to conscience, it is clear that the situation today is acutely difficult. How do the ideals of brotherly love, justice, honesty, and service to truth fare not only when pitted against the perennial weaknesses of the human animal, but within the environment of Xerox machines, computers, television, sophisticated neuro-chemicals, electronic banking, word-processors, multinational corporations, genetic engineering, and the thousands upon thousands of technological innovations that have appeared and are appearing every day in every pocket of life?

To what extent are these innovations a help, and to what extent are they a hindrance to living as a human being? Improved external conditions of living?—no doubt, although this may be questioned when taking the long view, of course. But increasingly, modern people faced with this new culture, this new external life, find more and more an internal emptiness, a confusion, a gnawing question as to whether they are living at all—or simply *being* lived by all the inventions of modern man.

It is an extremely complex question. 1984 is almost here and it is neither bad in the way that had been feared, nor good in the way that had been hoped. For example, the life of the family has been assaulted on all sides by numerous factors: new economic structures toppling the vocational identities of men and women, new techniques of birth control offering women a new independence, new psychological and religious teachings stripping away the behavioral constraints of the past, forces within education and the entertainment/communications industry replacing familial roles of authority in matters of conduct for children. Yet the family has not disappeared, neither as an ideal nor as an external fact in modern life. What has appeared, however, is the rather clear awareness that we do not know what, actually, the family is for, or what it ever was for.

The same is true in many other areas of life. The problem of leisure made it clear that the old values of hard work were not going to fade away; on the contrary. But who knows, exactly, *why* hard work (not oppressive work) is of value? Perhaps not even our immediate forefathers knew, even though they praised it so often.

Modern educators attempted to do away with certain demands on young people's attention and memory. It didn't work, and now there are as many educators seeking to go back to strict academic discipline as there are those who continue experiments in the affective domain and beyond. But as to what education should produce within the growing person and as to why discipline is necessary for real learning, no one knows anymore.

The problem as it exists in the field of education is quite instructive. In the West, the liberal education movement arose in the last century with the avowed purpose of widening the scope of human inquiry through making all ideas and teachings available to everyone. Through the new technology of printing, published material of every sort began to become available and the literacy level of modern man began its spectacular rise. Prior to this, the average man was considerably more in contact, emotionally, with the specific traditional teaching in which his life was immersed. Although his acceptance of religious authority was usually uncritical, he nevertheless retained in some measure the *will*, the emotional force, to live according to great ideals and values. He was more in relationship to his body and his feelings.

As the modern era progressed, such a state of affairs came to be regarded as constricting and blindly accepting. It was thought necessary to develop the intellect of man. But how to develop the intellect of man without unwittingly creating a buffer between the mind and the heart? What was not seen was that for certain ideas a definite preparation of the emotions and the body is necessary if these ideas are to have their intended beneficial action upon man. Nor was it considered that through this process of making all ideas available to everyone (without exact knowledge of the conditions under which such ideas need to be presented), men and women were being drawn more and more into their thoughts, and moving further and further away from the life of feeling and natural instinct, wherein reside the most powerful energies of the human organism.

Widespread questioning of authority accompanied the stimulated appetite for mental information and explanations, having its immediate effect on political authority throughout the Western world, and soon reaching to the areas of religious and family life as well. Above all, this process was fueled by the development of modern science with its specific canons of knowing and its particular view of reality. Everyone can and should know everything, can and should pass judgment on everything—from the nature of the universe to the actions of the king to the decisions of the father and the mother. That this right and ability to know and evaluate demanded a harmonious development of all the parts of the human structure was completely ignored—or, at best, acknowledged only in theory.

Almost all the changes which are visiting us now show this same pattern. Those who want to go back to old forms do not know what exactly was valuable about the old forms; those who want to go forward with the help of the extraordinary new technologies do so without knowing what is their good. To stay with the example of education, if the aim of education is to retain the child's integrity of body, mind, and feeling while informing the young person about the world around him, then it is absurd to offer young people discipline or concepts in a manner that furthers their inner fragmentation. For example, although love of neighbor is a greater value than egoistic pleasure, it is absurd to teach about love with methods that induce egoistic fear and which thereby make the human being structurally incapable of love even while he is being persuaded that he must love. It is the same with all the values of human existence.

Therefore, the problem is not the content of our beliefs in the modern world. It is the fragmentation of our nature, the forcing of all man's psychic power into one small region of his being, from which it is impossible for him to act as a whole individual. The problem is enormously complicated by the tendency to believe we must be achieving value or happiness when we are getting what we want—complicated because the technological process gives us the content of what we want while at the same time forcing our consciousness into a small segment of our total organic structure.

The automatizing process of technology—technology makes things easy, makes things possible—is what needs the most careful scrutiny. What used to be done with difficulty, or what used to be considered impossible, is now done with ease. People communicate over long distances, see each other over long distances, read writings that were never before available, travel to places all over the world, etc., etc. And in all this we persuade ourselves that the pleasure and gratification of these new abilities should be the satisfaction of our whole being. It is not so, and the increasing neuroses of modern people are ample testimony to that. All the other parts of our nature unconsciously go unfed, and the whole of ourselves grows progressively more lopsided and unbalanced, even while we are being persuaded that we are getting what all have always wanted.

Materialism as such is therefore not the problem. It is the crowding of our sense of self into a fragment of our total structure, and this is a process that goes on unnoticed.

Mechanization as such is not the problem, although many critics of the modern era imagine it is. The fact is that there are parts of our nature that are mechanical and that are meant to be mechanical—and these parts include a part of the mind and emotional nature, as well as the physical, moving aspects of our being. The problem is the self-deception that appears when we try to wring higher feelings and a sense of purpose out of these parts of ourselves that have no inherent relation to purpose, consciousness, and universal value, parts of ourselves that are designed to serve, as *good* servants, the more alive elements of the mind. These lower parts, let us remember, were carefully designated by Plato as what he called "the tradesman" of the outer and inner Republic, a notion developed even more fully in the ancient teaching about caste in India.

The pull of the outer world is now, and has surely always been, the pull toward the mechanical parts of our nature. And the proscriptions and warnings about the outer world, the world of the senses, has always been, at root, a warning against the all-too-human tendency to disperse the whole of one's inner force in these mechanical parts. Through this dispersion the higher in man remains undeveloped forever. Man loses his soul while gaining the world.

It would be absurd, and certainly not inherently necessary, to try to turn back the clock to reproduce more difficult conditions of living, as though such difficulties by themselves would bring man back to his full potentialities and inner morality. On the contrary, artificially produced difficulties often have the tendency to keep man even more strongly directed away from his own real inner force through the emotional fascination and egoistic satisfactions of achievements that have no real, deeply understood meaning in life. Witness the sense of hopelessness and despair of many people who, with extraordinary dedication and sacrifice, undergo great difficulties above and beyond the powers of ordinary people and who, like the rest of us, ultimately end by asking "why?", "what is it all for?"

The sense that it is something in ourselves which needs to be attended to is what spurred the development of modern psychology in the early part of this century. But without the eternal truths of the great traditions to guide them, psychologists failed to identify the parts of the human nature that actually can achieve value and moral power in life. The vision of human wholeness offered by modern psychology thus fell far short of the real integrity that is offered to man as a possibility. The lesser unities—the happiness, self-reliance, and adjustment to life which psychology offered—did not have the crystallized power to withstand the pulls of outer life, the present automatizing effects of technology in our culture. Therapeutic success was not as strong as the forces of our culture and so even the most mentally healthy among us now suffer the same sense of inner emptiness as the rest of the modernized world. Far more is needed within the being of man to meet and master the movements of inner force toward the mechanical parts of human nature where they are sectioned off and fragmented. Plato's ruling principle within man, the spirit, the higher mind, was not found by psychology—of course, it was not even sought.

Now, all around us, new teachings—or old teachings in new places—come forward speaking about these higher, more inner elements of the mind. Psychology itself is turning to these new religions of the ancient East and West. Teachings and methods are appearing which may actually bring man into contact with more inner forces, higher sensations and emotions.

Yet the influence of technology on society increases, accelerates more rapidly than ever before. The pull outward is greater than ever before—that is, the pull to make use of these new developments, new inventions. In fact, it is impossible to live at all in the present world without devoting most of one's working hours to the results of these new technologies, both in the problems they solve and the problems they create.

What we are concerned with are the problems they create with respect to the art of living as a human being, a being ontologically structured as an inhabitant of two worlds, two levels. The great philosophies of all times have taught that just this is the perennial problem of human life—whether these two levels are signified by the dichotomy rational/animal (where rational refers to higher mind), Self/ego, or spirit/flesh. The problem is ancient, but the counters are very different today and need to be recognized as such. How to be toward *both* the new directions offered by ancient spiritual teachings now surfacing in our midst with bewildering rapidity, and the pull outward of powerful new technologies?

The fact of the matter is that changes in our external patterns of living are now so rapid and confusing that these same ancient spiritual traditions are often being selectively used to mask this confusion rather than understand its roots in our own structure as ontologically incomplete beings: its roots in our unseen mechanicalness, fragmentation, suggestibility, and uncertainty about what we are and what we were meant to become. It is still unclear how the traditions are going to respond to this tendency to use methods such as meditation for such purposes as dealing with the stress of modern living.

In this sense we are, all of us, at the same zero point. The representatives of tradition no less than the rest of us, stand in front of this perennial human question of how to be toward the two movements within the frame of man and the cosmos—the movement outward toward manifestation and the proliferation of new forms, and the movement inward toward unity.

To take spiritual methods for the purpose of making the outward movement more successful or comfortable is no less a deception than to promote external, cultural innovations as the answer to the inner problems of human life. This latter mirage is precisely what has led to the crushing tension and moral despair of the present era. The former mirage holds no better promise. To substitute the illusion of inner progress for the illusion of outer progress is still to remain blind to the needs of the two natures within us which, we are told, must both be given care if man is to live according to his real nature and possibilities.

Broadly generalizing, we may say that the crime of the Western world has been to emphasize the outward, involutionary movement to the neglect of the inward, evolutionary force. But the Eastern world is also guilty of a crime, converse of the West and no doubt of somewhat lesser visible effect: the excessive emphasis on the inward movement to the neglect not only of social conditions in its own lands, but of the psychospiritual needs of the rest of the world. Why has it taken the East so long to come forward with its teachings? The need for them has existed for many centuries. Why do they appear only when political and economic conditions make it physically necessary for Eastern spiritual leaders to come to the West? Why were they not watching us and sending help long ago? Is this a sign that even the help they are now sending may be insufficient or inaccurately designed to penetrate the specific subjectivity of contemporary Western man?

The agonizing problems of social injustice illustrate this point about the need for man to care for both sides of his nature. Ancient systems of hierarchical social organization at their root offered all human beings the deep fundamental respect due to the inner divinity of human nature. This respect for all men and women was, ideally, embodied in the exact rituals and rules of living proper to every social class within the complex organization of a civilization. In a truly traditional society, this profound respect for human nature would be far more than a slogan or an ideal; it would be written into the physical and emotional habits of the culture. But mankind seems to have forgotten the real meaning of self-respect. And having forgotten this most important element, the social forms that were meant to support it gradually began to function as instruments of oppression and egoism. The whole aim of the social order became equated with the aims of the ego. At its best, society was looked upon as therapeutic, rather than transformational.

It was inevitable that people would begin to believe that the outer form caused the inner state. The modern world has witnessed the clear perception by every unprivileged social class of the absence of respect for self: ethnic minorities, the economically exploited, women, and many others. To achieve the only form of self-respect which the society understood, all classes expend their energy toward changing the external system. But this does not and has not brought about the inner well-being of people.

Here again the new technologies offer their power—but in the service of what? New economic and financial structures have been made possible by scientific technology in its vast scale of ramifications through new forms of communication, transportation, warfare, agriculture, development and exploitation of raw materials, internationalism, etcetera.

There is no hierarchy left, no sense of any inherent difference between people. And surely no one who has seen the ends to which hierarchical structures have been employed in the modern world can possibly complain or seek to turn back the clock.

Yet is there not, after all, a difference between people that has nothing to do with social, economic, or ethnic class? Here again, as with Plato, we begin from zero. All the classifications of human beings that we know have either been perverted to fanatical ends or, like those of modern psychology, have faded away into irrelevance. Yet the question is crucial; we may say that it is the most crucial question of all. Crucial because our way of thinking about it will determine where we turn for guidance in living. Assuming, of course, that we wish to turn to people for guidance and not to technology.

Please do not smile; it is entirely possible for people to look to inanimate machines for guidance rather than to living ideas and wiser human beings. What else does it mean that modern man is at the mercy of the present cultural crisis, hypnotically dazed by all the changes going on around him? All our psychic force is given to reactions of fear or enthusiasm: fear that some mystery essential to human life is about to be lost forever due to the encroachment of new technologies; enthusiasm that a totally understood world, a new age is just around the corner.

Our philosophy, such as it is, is actually being given to us by our machines! Which is tantamount to saying that the external world, the world of the senses (in the ancient language), is dictating to the world of the mind and the heart. Recall, for example, that science was born from the impulse to know the truth for oneself, free of the tyranny of dogmatic beliefs and hypocritical, life-killing moral strictures. Unfortunately, the intellectual methods for solving localized scientific questions—methods which produced great discoveries about the external world—soon became the touchstone for the solution of all the problems of human life, problems which can only be solved by the integration of body, mind, and feeling in man, rather than by the intellect alone.

Now, in the present moment, when the technical solution to an external problem appears, people turn to the technical solution for moral guidance as well. Let us ask ourselves, how have new inventions in the areas of computer technology, space exploration, birth control, or electronic communications influenced our understanding of what man is, of what the mind is, of what caring relationships are, of what we owe our children, of what life and death are, of what a genuine nurturing environment for the growth of a human being is, this latter phrase being, quite exactly, the very definition of culture?

But as with our dependence on scientific intellection, it is clear that guidance means nothing if it does not also direct us toward awakening the faculty within ourselves that can actually experience value within reality. Science was unable to give us that not because what it taught was false, but because it could not teach us how to tend to the formation within ourselves of an inner unity or moral force.

The great philosophies of the past arose from within remarkable human beings who could give voice to the ideas necessary for moral development, ideas that could guide men toward discovering for themselves the whole truth about both the inner and outer condition of human life on earth. The origin of real philosophy is not the intellectual imitation of external reality, but the outer expression of truths about an invisible world perceived through what the traditions call "the eye of the heart." Great philosophy—that is, great guidance for man—comes, let us be blunt about it, from men of greater being.

Where and who are they now? Who are the people that can guide us in the present situation? Will we find them among the gurus who have come to the West? among our scientists? our professors? our priests?—or do they perhaps exist among our artists—painters, writers, sculptors, composers, or in the world of film, dance, theater? Are there men and women who live at the cutting edge of cultural revolution without being swallowed by it and believing in it?

Once again: the zero point. For on the human scale what does it actually mean, levels of being? Intellectual brilliance, artistic talent, robes of office, great learning, kindness, even genius and saintliness—what do these terms mean anymore? Do they really point to that decisive element within man that brings both a vision of truth and the practical means to transmit it to others without creating in us yet more confusion, fragmentation, or wishful thinking?

Of course, of equal importance is a question we have not yet asked: How do we, who stand in need of guidance, search for it? What do we demand of ourselves in this search?

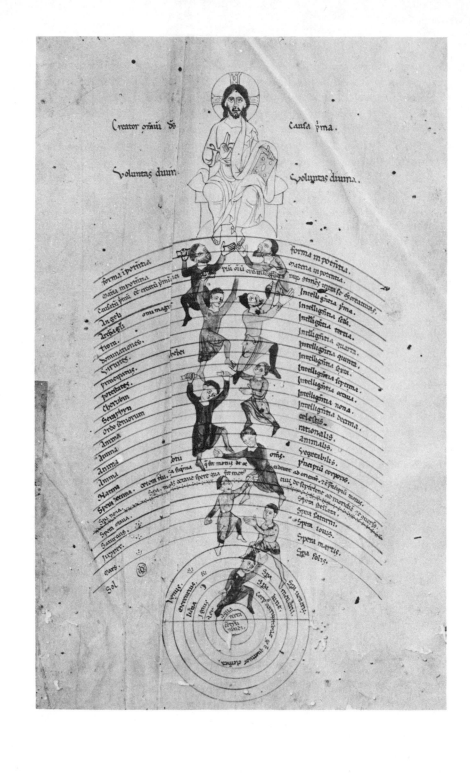

Creator omniū ds̄   causa p̄ma.

Voluntas diuin.   Voluptas diuina.

forma ipotentia.   forma in potentia.
                                    materia in potentia.
gratia increata.
Causatū boni et creatū p̄mi ser.   vap̄ omnes inter se. gerant.us
Angeli   omi magn   Intelligentia p̄ma.
Archangeli   Intelligentia scd̄a.
tiona.   Intelligentia tertia.
dominationes.   Intelligentia quarta.
Virtutes   hebet   Intelligentia quinta.
p̄ncipatus.   Intelligentia sexta.
potestates.   Intelligentia septima.
Cherubin   Intelligentia octaua.
Seraphyn   Intelligentia nona.
ordo demonum   Intelligentia decima.
Anima   celestis.
Anima   rationalis.
Anima   motu.   animalis.
Anima   fsta ista mā. omi. uegetabilis.
Natura.   p̄ncipiū corporis.
Spera p̄ma.   oriom̄ tali...   adeut ad oriente.
Spera nona.   Spera. molt.   eius de septrione...
Spera octaua.   Spera stellata.
Spera.saturni.   Spera saturni.
Jupiter.   Spera iouis.
                                  Spera martis.
Mars   Spera solis.
Sol.
          Venus.   Spera uener.
     Mercurius.   Spera mercurii.
     Luna.   Spera lune.
     Ignis.   corp. corruptibile.
     Aer.
     Aqua   terra
     Terra   corpus inuisi.
          De materia diuina

THE SEARCH FOR A WISE MAN

1

THERE exists in the Bibliothèque Nationale in Paris an anonymous twelfth-century Hermetic manuscript containing two remarkable illustrations of the cosmic scheme as envisioned by Christianity. Like many such diagrams which have come down to us from the prescientific era, they show a universe created on the principles of conscious emanation and gradations of reality symbolized by concentric circles with the earth at the center and the creator enthroned above the highest, outermost sphere. What is unusual about these two pictures, however, is that unlike most familiar representations of the so-called geocentric universe, they have superimposed upon them a number of human figures, each placed at different levels between the person of Christ above, and the earth below. Even more striking is the fact that each of these human figures holds his hand outstretched to the one above him.

These diagrams may be generally said to illustrate the ascent of the soul. But to a modern person searching for self-knowledge and self-development, they can communicate a rather special idea, also shared by all the great spiritual traditions of the past: the growth of man's being is somehow coordinate with the very structure of the universe; psychological change, in its deepest and most basic sense, is not merely a subjective process that takes place apart from the laws of nature. On the contrary, it too occurs according to objective laws, the same laws by which the world we see, as well as the worlds we cannot see, are born, preserved, and destroyed. The evolution of consciousness is both a cosmic fact and a human possibility. Therefore, in a fundamental sense, the development of man's being is meant to follow a track already laid down for him in the makeup of reality. Such is the traditional idea.

If we wish to understand the nature of the wise man, or the spiritual guide, there is much help to be gotten from this cosmic perspective offered us by tradition. Through this perspective, we may also gain some insight into the particular difficulties and opportunities which the contemporary seeker faces, confronted by a bewildering variety of new religious movements and by the fact that in our time and place all of the ancient spiritual traditions seem to be converging upon us, sending emissaries to the modern world from realms of thought and experience hitherto relatively separate from each other and unknown to modern man.

Let us look more closely at these illustrations. In both cases we note that among the figures placed at different levels of being there are several whose faces are directed not upwards, toward Christ, but downwards, toward those human beings at the lower levels of ascent. Why? Why are they not directing their attention, like the others, toward the ultimate goal—liberation from the spheres of the world, and union with God? Surely, this is an indication that not only is there a track laid down for the seeker in the very structure of reality, but also that reality contains in its essence a factor of care for man. Having said that, however, it is necessary to emphasize that the man to whom this care is directed is he who has already left earth, whose hand is stretched upward.

What emerges here is a picture of *a sacred universe* far from the popular modern clichés about the static and narrow medieval Christian cosmic scheme. One has only to enter a Gothic cathedral with a more needful attention to understand something of what is being depicted in these illustrations. The Medieval cathedral was nothing less than a model of the universe. What we appreciate as the beauty of the cathedral was, to the originators of the cathedral, the representation of that element in reality which can attract the human heart toward God. The cathedral, the universe, is fundamentally a place in which man is to seek God and *in which God is able to be sought.* Yet this same cathedral, this model of the universe, was built on the basis of a renewed discovery of the interrelationship between the symbolism of geometry and the teachings of religion. The true dynamism of the cosmos, its *vertical dynamism,* is visible only to the man who is in the act of reaching upward. This dynamism has to do with the deep interrelationship between universal laws of nature and the transformations of being toward and away from ultimate Being. Care for man lies at the heart of reality; but to be cared for, man must seek. This is not only a psychological, but a mathematical law.

And thus our attention comes to rest on what are for us the most significant aspects of these illustrations. In each case there is one and only one figure who is not only looking downwards, but who has also grasped the outstretched hand of the man beneath him. This relationship does not occur at the upper levels of progression, nor does it obtain at the very lowest stages. It occurs not quite halfway up through the spheres.

At first glance, one is tempted to think of this particular figure—the only one who is both looking downwards and also grasping the hand of the man ascending beneath him—as the paradigm of the spiritual teacher. But all the relationships in the diagrams need to be considered in this context, although space does not allow that we do so here. Nevertheless, it is apparent that the care for man which is coordinate with the structure of the cosmos is not to be understood too quickly as some general force, some general arrangement of the elements of reality. Something rather more specific seems to be depicted: namely, that *cosmic care for man (who seeks) exists in the form of guidance and help through the instrumentality of other human beings.*

It should be pointed out that we might have gone to any number of traditional sources for this idea, once we have discovered how to look for it. In the traditions of Asia the spiritual guide is understood to be what we might describe in Western language as the incarnation on earth of the supreme metaphysical reality. And his relationship to his disciples is understood to be an incarnation or reflection in miniature of the manner in which the absolute creates, destroys, maintains, and reabsorbs into itself the whole of the universal order. *"Guru is Brahman"* (the absolute), is too hastily interpreted by many Westerners as implying some preposterous overestimation of the spiritual guide in Hinduism, and is equally misunderstood as being only a figure of speech. It is truer to the traditional meaning of this formula to approach it from the direction we are discovering in our Hermetic/Christian illustrations. Brahman is he who *teaches.* Such *teaching* is not, of course, the mere expression of verbal formulations, but is an ontological process, obeying specific universal laws, having to do with the origination and development of energies.

In Mahayana Buddhism the Buddha (The Awakened) is also understood ontologically and psychologically as the manifestation in the world of relative reality of the supreme Truth-of-Being (Emptiness). This doctrine is developed with particular power and clarity in the Tibetan traditions through the concept of the *tulku,* the incarnated lama who is a manifestation of a universal principle for the sake of all creatures living in the world of illusion. Spiritual transformation, as well as the transmission of the teaching, is here also understood in terms of the unfolding within man and among the spiritual brotherhood of the highest cosmic forces.

This same general teaching is to be found in Judaism as well. The conventional (or so-called mainstream) interpretations of the Old Testament, with their formulations concerning the absolute separation of God and creature, would never lead one to suspect this fact. In *The Zohar,* the principal text of the Kabbalah, we find the idea given as one among several readings of the first words of Genesis, "In the beginning God created the heaven and the earth." And in various places in *The Zohar* the wise man is described as the very life of the universe.

But what are all these traditions saying to modern man in search of himself?

Specifically, they are telling us that the wise man and his actions, his teaching, have to be approached in terms of *events at the level of being*, and not simply as *events at the level of psyche*. A man who is psychologically great may be, shall we say, ontologically ordinary. Our concept of the superior man, our model of human wisdom and goodness is seriously challenged by this traditional concept of the cosmic nature of the teacher. To appreciate this challenge fully, it is necessary to consider also an exceedingly important corollary which goes to the heart of our main subject: *If the spiritual guide and his teaching concern events at the level of being,* then we must also say that *the search for a teacher must also be an event at the level of being* and not merely or solely an event at the level of psyche.

Such ideas are going to throw into question the quality of modern man's own search, no matter how intense and sincere it seems to be. At the same time, however, a deeper kind of hope is to be found in this perspective, a hope that links the authentic search to the universe itself and which, in terms of our own possibilities as individuals, does not require of us the kind of heroic efforts that we habitually expend and which lead us nowhere. Another kind of demand upon the seeker will become visible, in its way a far greater and more difficult demand, but at the same time one that can be met by that in man which is the instrument of a real, fundamental energy of ascent.

Our Christian/Hermetic illustrations of the cosmos have brought us toward a rather new way of looking at the whole issue of the search for a teacher. But they have done so only by placing us in front of a great enigma—the distinction between psyche and being; between what I feel, what I desire, what I believe, think, perceive, sense, and imagine—and what *I am.*

Yet, in fact, although this formulation brings us to the edge of a profound mystery, by itself it cannot take us very far. Mystery, enigma, paradox—secret: these are words whose real sense lies in very ancient realms. Modern man has not invented these terms and therefore we who are trying to understand the real issues involved in the search for a spiritual guide must not be too dependent on our modern habitual understanding.

The mystery of *being,* like every great mystery of the eternal teachings, is not simply an intellectual puzzle, nor even necessarily a problem to be solved. Nor are such mysteries to be identified exclusively with the sort of sense of the profound and holy which we may often feel in front of the great forces of nature, although these experiences come much closer to the point if we know how to analyze them.

We must recognize that a spiritual mystery does more than thwart the intellect—it breaks down the emotions as well; it causes suffering of a very special sort; it is unbearable in a very lawful way.

So let us reformulate our question in a way that can bring us closer to the impact of the traditional teachings about the universe and man, being and psyche. This we can do by changing only one word in our formulation—but what an extraordinary difference this one word will make! And we shall see that through this minor change, which actually implies a completely transformed sense of the question, a new direction for thought stretches out before us, one which we can trust to guide our reflections about the current spiritual crisis.

The distinction between psyche and being must be approached as the distinction between what I feel, what I desire, what I believe, think, perceive, sense, and imagine—and *whether* I am, whether *I* exist at all.

On the one hand, there are the phenomena of my psychic life—my feelings of satisfaction or dissatisfaction, my efforts to explain, my reactions of pleasure or anxiety, my impulse to know and find out, my interest in people or ideas, my judgments, my intellectual and emotional associations, my hopes and fears, attractions and repulsions. But on the other hand, there is the completely different question of the reality of my own being.

In the contemporary era, the first glimpse of the cosmic, trans-psychological nature of the spiritual process came with the introduction of the teachings of Zen Buddhism. In the accounts offered by D. T. Suzuki of the transactions between Zen master and pupil, one began to feel the great scale of this process. The teacher was seeking to create in the pupil an event on the level of being. And this not only in pupils or monks already committed to the spiritual quest, but those approaching the teacher for the first time.

A tremendous hope was being offered here to modern, Western man. Many of these stories of first encounter with the master presented the picture of a man, whose own search was merely psychological, suddenly having created in himself an event on the level of being, an internal event in which his whole psychology was for a moment undermined (that is, transcended).

In the Zen tradition, this experience had to do with something that, as it was put, went beyond words, beyond the intellect, was not explainable by reason, irrational. The Zen experience made it difficult for the pupil to adjust the event into his sense of self, his ego.

It began to be understood that through a teacher one may discover not the answers to emotional or intellectual problems, but rather the experience of a search for oneself beyond the level of psychology. The transaction between Zen master and pupil was felt to be on a completely different scale than the familiar conception of the transactions between priest and believer, educator and student, psychiatrist and patient.

In effect, the master was—to return for a moment to our cosmic diagrams—pulling the pupil up by his hair.

There was no question here of beginning the search for a teacher rightly or wrongly. It was to be understood that it could not begin rightly. No need to worry about the right criteria for a teacher, no need to concern oneself about his credentials.

For how *could* a search begin rightly? One is a beginner, one knows a great deal and understands nothing; life is a painful confusion composed not only of sufferings and frustrations, but of hopes and impulses that lead nowhere and that appear shamefully trivial in front of the occasionally glimpsed fact of death. One must inevitably approach a teacher in the wrong way.

Yet the main thing was to approach a teacher! And if the teacher was a teacher the event on the level of being would be created in the seeker. But could the seeker accept this event? Could he allow it to have the necessary action upon him? Or would he instead run away by turning once again to his psychology (his intellectual or emotional habits) in a way that prevented the event from having its action?

The problem of selecting the right teacher, or of finding an authentic teacher—problems which figure so largely in the contemporary spiritual situation—never seemed to arise in this body of literature. In any case, they did not arise with the poignancy that characterizes the modern situation.

And this is quite understandable. After all, this material comes from a culture of basically one central religious thrust—Buddhism; and a culture in which, in general, the channels that lead to the spiritual teacher are well-marked and established within the culture itself.

It is only in the contemporary world that the element of choice is so predominant. We may presume that in the traditional civilization, it was not a question of selecting a teacher or a tradition from among a shelf of varied offerings: It was rather a question of approaching a teacher and then seeing what happened.

If the material from Zen has an immediate relevance to the present situation, it is surely to tell us that the question of selecting, choosing, judging, weighing, determining for oneself who is or who is not a real teacher may be understood in a right or a wrong way and may in fact be an actual obstacle in finding a teacher.

And this too is quite understandable the moment one asks, what in myself is to be trusted to see rightly the qualities of this or that person?

Thus the literature of Zen provides a special meaning to the idea of the spiritual teacher's credentials. Like every tradition, Zen maintains a rigorous rule of transmission by which "the robe of the master" is handed down to the true successor. But it is *only* in the encounter between the teacher and the seeker that the meaning of these credentials is understood.

The sacred books of the East are replete with treatises enumerating the qualities which an authentic teacher must possess. He must be compassionate, must have perfect knowledge of the teaching, must be "God-realized"—the list can be very long indeed. But what is a modern person, or for that matter any person who has not yet entered an authentic path, to make of these qualities? What we ordinarily understand as compassion or knowledge may have no useful relationship to what such terms mean within the action of the tradition itself.

There is a Zen story which very well illustrates what is entailed in approaching and testing the Master. It concerns a famous samurai warrior who enters the chambers of a Zen Master, saying, "I have heard that you know the secret of heaven and hell. Please instruct me!"

The teacher looks up at the warrior, bedecked in his magnificent armor, his head held high. "Who are you?" the Master asks, without much interest.

"I am a *samurai*!"

The Master laughs at him. "You?" he says, with an air of incredulity. "You a samurai? Don't make me spew!"

At this, the great warrior's face darkens; he instantly draws out his gleaming sword and in a fury lunges forward to bring it down upon the Master's head.

"*There* open the gates of hell," says the Master, looking directly into the warrior's eyes.

The samurai freezes, his arm arrested in mid-air. In a moment of intense self-seeing, where all his pride and egoism stand nakedly revealed to him, he silently bows his head and slowly replaces his sword. He stands there, head down, not moving.

Quietly, the Master says: "And there open the gates of heaven."

* * *

One can regard this story from many points of view, but for our purposes it is a lesson concerning the inner event which a teacher calls forth. Did the warrior have a preconceived idea of what it meant to learn, or what kind of knowledge a spiritual master possesses? All of that is washed away in the moment he sees his own weakness.

The event on the level of being is not his anger before he sees; it is not even his shame, which is only a reaction to what he has seen. The real event is the seeing itself. Everything else only exists on the level of psyche, that is, it is under the sway of thought-associations, images of self and world which are little more than fantasies, but which have captured all the real energy of presence within the man.

The stories of the Zen tradition almost always concern the release of this mysterious energy of the self which until then has been captured by mental or emotional patterns within the psyche of man. The recognition of this pure energy by the ego produces a shock of recognition, often joyous, in which the "I" that has been suffering for so long to affirm its being suddenly recognizes what is its source and real being.

For a moment, the psyche understands and accepts that it has no basic reality, except as an effect or servant (to use Western religious language) of the real, the higher—perhaps the word "God" may be introduced in this context.

We have been speaking of a cosmic track, a path built into the very structure of the universe. The impact of the tradition of Zen, even that portion of the tradition which has been brought to America, was in part to destroy all interpretations of religious symbolism that had become fixed in the psychic patterns of the ego.

To many Westerners, Zen was a breath of fresh air, to say the least, confirming that something had gone terribly wrong in our relationship to the symbols and practices of Christianity and Judaism. The cosmos had been turned over to the scientists and the whole idea of mystery was therewith reduced to something which man could never understand, something external. God was above, man was below. By finding a comfortably fixed place for the mystery of God, man was given free reign to live in his psyche, going, so to say, once a week to the "church" of hope, belief, and good thoughts. By divesting the world in which he actually lived of symbolic power, by taking the cosmos literally, by seeing war, for example, as only what it appeared to be, by seeing one's house and family as only what they appeared to be—that is to say, by failing to search for a relationship to the forces of being at work in the whole environment of life—man became an atheist in fact, no matter what religious beliefs occupied the neighborhood church in his mind.

Zen confirmed the moribund quality of many modern people's relationship to the symbolism of Western religions. But it did so not through any philosophical nihilism, nor any negative criticism of religion—but mainly by indicating, through extraordinarily powerful examples of human relationship, the relationship of teacher and pupil, that an event, a tangible perceptible happening was possible, an event within the self that exposed for what they ..e all dreams and fantasies, all self-induced mysticism, all interesting intellectual explanations, all comforting notions of life or no life after death.

It was not long, however, before the formulations of Zen began to be blended in with the humanism of the twentieth century, particularly the teachings of modern psychology. Although the blending of modern psychology with aspects of spiritual teachings has in the seventies perhaps helped many people lead happier, more productive lives, it has in the main buffered the metaphysical impact of these teachings.

Cosmic symbolism, it seems, cannot be abandoned forever by man in search of transformation. In its traditional setting, of course, Zen Buddhism by no means abandons such symbolism, which exists in the manifestation of its art, the submission to exact ritual, and in the contents of the scriptures. But with its emphasis on meditation, Zen recognizes that symbolic forms may have no real action on man unless he is in an inner state which allows the symbol to penetrate beneath the level of the mental and emotional associations, beneath the level of the psyche.

The blending of spiritual expressions and modern humanistic, psychological techniques usually prevents this process, either because the exact nature of the requisite inner state is not understood or because the symbols and methods of a tradition are altered in order to be acceptable to the psyche. Thus the experience of a purer energy within the self is either never reached or, if it is reached through various adapted spiritual methods, it immediately recombines with the associations in the psyche in a manner that goes unrecognized by anyone.

In the Hindu tradition, notably in the *Bhagavad Gita,* the cosmic symbolism of the path of transformation is so strongly expressed that even a modern reader senses the exalted nature of man's possible movement toward being. In this text, the difficulty of entering into this movement of the transformation of being is specifically described in terms of the encounter between the seeker, the warrior Arjuna, and the Guru, Krishna, God-Who-Teaches. Commensurate with the vast metaphysical framework of the teaching and nature of Krishna is the vastness of the struggle demanded of the seeker—here spoken of in terms of a great war of clashing armies within one many-branched family (the individual person).

Whereas what we are familiar with as Zen communicates the event at the level of being by stripping away every kind of self-identification with psychic contents, the familiar Hindu texts, like those of many traditions, use instead the method of mythic language, language that comprises images which are familiar and instantly felt by the individual, but which are made to resonate, so to say, within the interstices of familiar emotional associations. Unlike discursively formulated dogmas, where mystery is relegated to what simply cannot be understood, mythic language exerts extraordinary pressure on man through a predetermined double impact: it cannot be understood, but at the same time it must be understood. Myth is a call to engage more fully in the drama of life; dogmatic mystery, on the other hand, encourages the comfortable dualism of preestablished limits to what can be known and experienced.

It is said that all religious literature is but a portent and a reflection of what must be lived through in the existential spiritual process. As in this essay we are examining the search for a wise man and the nature of the pupil-teacher encounter, we can conclude that the pressure of myth has its three-dimensional reality in the pressure placed upon the pupil in the presence of the teacher. The pupil cannnot understand, but must understand.

The encounter with the teacher is experienced by the pupil as a call to engage in the play of forces which make up the drama of life. This is distinguished from the play of reactions which make up the lesser drama of the psychological associations within the mind. For example, when thought meets the resistance of a contrary thought, insight, a broader, reconciling thought, may appear. But an entirely different scale of reality is at issue when the impulse to be is met by the resistance of thought itself as it sucks in the precious energy of presence that is denoted by the word "I" in every traditional language. In that encounter with the forces of dispersal and absorption (the Hindu "attachment"), there lies the possible birth of the new being, the greater "I," *atman*, which is God in all things.

The Hindu tradition is rich in examples indicating that to be a pupil is as demanding as the cosmos is great. It would after all be a ludicrous contradiction if, after indicating the trans-psychological scale of the stages of man's possible being, it were then made to seem easy for an individual human being actually to enter the path. The great warrior Arjuna himself struggles against the demand that Krishna places upon him in the very first chapter of the *Bhagavad Gita*, a struggle which one insightful commentator has termed "the yoga of the dejection of Arjuna."[1]

What it entails to be an authentic pupil is tellingly illustrated in the sixteenth-century Hindu treatise, the *Vedantasara* ("The Essence of the Doctrines of Vedanta") summarized by Heinrich Zimmer in *Philosophies of India*. The list of requirements which the potential pupil must satisfy is truly awesome, being in every respect comparable to the equally awesome criteria which are established for the authentic teacher.

Just as the teacher must be perfect in his knowledge, so the pupil must be perfect in his wish for knowledge.

> Just as a man carrying on his head a load of wood that has caught fire would go rushing to a pond to quench the flames, even so should the adhikarin (the "competent student"), scorched with the mad pains of the fire of life in the world, its birth, its death, its self-deluding futility, go rushing to a guru learned in the Vedas, who, himself having reached the goal of Vedanta, now abides serene in uninterrupted consciousness of the essence of imperishable being. The adhikarin is to come to this guru bearing presents in his hand, ready to serve, and prepared to obey in every way.[2]

But this is only the beginning. The treatise goes on to require of the prospective pupil that he already have a general comprehension of all the main written teachings, that he have pursued his life rigorously adhering to all outer forms of the general religion, including the practice of "special austerities that conduce to the expiation of sin, and all of the usual orthodox meditations designed to conduce to the concentration of the mind."

Here we are touching on the subject of the necessary preparation of the pupil, and the indispensable role played in this preparation by the cultural and moral fabric of the traditional society.

In his introduction to the life of Tibet's great saint, Milarepa, the contemporary Tibetan scholar Lobsang Lhalungpa speaks directly to this issue:

> (The Vajrayana training) is thus a process of psychological transformation. . . . From the outset, one works to free oneself from all superstitious complexes of superiority or inferiority based on sex, race, color, or creed. A deeper sense of one entire human family and universal fellowship is to be developed as the foundation for a right attitude to human relationships. Only then is the seeker led toward a process of spiritualization . . . This psychological reorientation, which is the basic aim of all true culture, embraces the totality of factors and forces that go to make up an individual's whole stream of being and his attitude toward life . . . Without this preparatory development of a sound and sane basic atti-

tude toward the goals of living, the whole spiritual endeavor is susceptible to egoistic self-love . . .[3]

This Hindu treatise presents the picture of the fully prepared pupil
who has lived to the full the sufferings and joys of a normal human life,
but who longs for something more real than even the best that normal
life can bring. The treatise goes on to list an astonishing array of powers
and virtues which even the best-informed Westerner would have imagined to be attributes of one already far along the path itself. For example, the pupil must have an attitude that "keeps the mind from being
troubled by sense objects—the only sense activity permitted to the student . . . being that of listening eagerly to the words of his guru." The
student must have made "a decisive turning away" from "the entire system of the outer world." He must have "the power to endure without the
slightest discomposure extremes of heat and cold, weal and woe, honor
and abuse, loss and gain." He must have the power of "constant concentration of the mind."

> His (the neophyte's) heart and mind must already have been cleansed
> by the preliminary rituals and austerities of the orthodox religious
> practices of his community. He must be sufficiently trained in the Holy
> Scriptures. And he must then be able to bring himself to gain possession
> of these "necessary means" for the transcending of illusion. "Such an as-
> pirant," we read, "is a qualified student."[4]

It is necessary, of course, to ask after the principle behind these formulations. When taken too literally, they would simply place the possible encounter with a teacher out of reach of most modern people, who,
far from having intentionally worked to the limits of any traditional orthodoxy, have not even been automatically prepared through the absorption of the values and impressions provided by a traditional cultural
environment.

Concerning this principle, that is, the meaning for us of these state-
ments about the high status of even beginning on the path of transformation, it is perhaps most important to recognize one rather clear fact
about what we are calling a "traditional cultural environment." Such an
environment is one in which, to some extent, the teachings are already
reaching out to people. Here we do not refer to those clearly marked
channels discussed above in connection with a tradition such as Zen existing in a cultural milieu where anyone who is sufficiently interested
can discover one or another form of intensive spiritual practice. We

mean something far broader and less defined—the art, the literature, the habits and customs, most of which, in a nonmodern culture, trace their origin, albeit often tortuously and in diluted fashion, to a central body of spiritual teachings.

What, then, is the principle we are seeking to discern? What actually is high about beginning on the path or recognizing the teacher? To answer that we have to ask more insistently about what it means that a teaching reaches out to man. How does it do this? And how could it do this today in an environment that has almost completely destroyed or replaced all the remnants of its own traditional core? Does what we are calling the event on the level of being depend so much on the cultural milieu? Or is it rather that for a teaching to be a living teaching and not solely a glorious but ineffective fossil, it must reach people exactly where they are and somehow make it possible for the *question*, the ontological event, to take place even in the depths of hell?

In short, can an authentic teacher appear and make it possible for modern man to recognize him? Who can pull us up by our hair?

We have reached the heart of our subject.

2

I have been trying to allow the traditional texts themselves to speak about one fundamental element in the relationship between teacher and pupil. I hope that something has come through concerning the mystery of the change of inner being which is offered man on the spiritual path.

A fuller treatment of this theme would have brought out many more aspects of our Christian/Hermetic diagram—for example, the astonishing notion that every creature beneath the level of God himself is a pupil of the higher. And this would have required us to consider as fully as possible the ancient idea that real human learning involves an exchange of energies and an interaction of forces identical in nature to the movement of forces by which the universe itself comes into being.

To do justice to the idea that it is man on the path who is actually higher man we might have gone to the legends and myths of the Teutons dealing with the struggles of the gods, which symbolize the effort toward spiritual liberation of man with greater understanding and being. Or we might have cited the traditions of ancient and medieval Iran, so profoundly illuminated by Henry Corbin, where it is said that only a man who possesses a soul, the body of light (a "subtle organism independent of his material organism"), can meet with and become the pupil of the Spiritual Guide.[5]

But space does not allow our dwelling any longer on these traditional formulas. We must now try to speak directly to the problem facing contemporary man in search of a guide. For that purpose we have perhaps drawn sufficient material from the traditions to serve as a counterweight to our habitual ways of thinking about this problem.

How does it stand, then, with the modern person "in search of a wise man"? The following is a phenomenological portrait which has been put together from direct observation of a large number of people, young and old, representing many walks of life. Included are also elements drawn from my own personal experience.

We must give our seeker a definite background of conventional religious experience. He has, at least once in his life, entered a church or synagogue in a condition of need. Let us say that he has gone directly to the priest or rabbi as well. He has laid his suffering before the altar of religion, in its modern, Western form.

Having entered in the state of need, he has come away with a strengthened religious personality. He has been given energy to face the doubt in himself and overcome it, to face the fear in himself and resist it; he takes arms against certain desires; a sense of belonging (whether to God or to the community) bolsters him against the emotions of self-pity and loneliness; a tincture of theology calms his restless intellect.

Having the strength now to face life, the future seeker soon runs head on into the worlds around him, the worlds of success and failure, of love and betrayal, of newspapers, television, and cinema, of books and art, of adventure, war, and human injustice, of ideologies, of sexual problems, psychiatrists, money worries, bodily pain, and physical inferiority. He discovers that he also has a political personality, a scientific personality, an artistic personality, a sexual personality, a vacation personality . . .

Thrown by life from one world into another, from one personality into another, he begins to sense the question "Who am I?", and reaches the conclusion that he does not know and that he must grow up and make his choice, take his stand.

He sees and yet does not see that this question is the most intimate aspect of his being. Everything in the life around him is urging him to find the answer, make a choice, define himself. But each attempt succeeds only for a while, until another of his personalities is activated. Again and again, the question arises in him—not simply, what shall I do? whom shall I marry? where shall I go?, but rather, who, what, is the being which calls itself by my name?

Even if he has already committed himself to a vocation, a spouse, an ideology—no matter. The world around him is not so committed; his cultural milieu offers no clear-cut values for him to accept or reject; always and in everything the carousel of his personalities turns and turns, and always he feels the pressure to know, to decide what he is, the pressure to solve the question of his being once and for all, and get on with living.

Turning again to religion, he finds—he does not know why—that it no longer helps. Or rather, it helps only for a while, like everything else. It speaks of the transcendent, of that which is deeper and higher than all the worlds he inhabits. Yet it is taken by him only in one of his many personalities. It urges him, like everything else in his life, to commit himself, to take his stand, make his choice. And he acknowledges the right of religion to make this demand upon him, upon his thinking and feeling.

But religion, which has tried hard to stay as strong as the world, has by this very fact remained as weak as the world. He blames himself and not religion, but the fact is that when again the intimate question "Who am I?" surges up in him he finds religion as but one item on the menu. It too wants to solve, that is to say, destroy, his question.

Is there something wrong with him? He considers psychotherapy and perhaps tries it for a while.

But it is too late for psychotherapy—he has already begun to read certain books containing ideas that make a new demand upon him, in the light of which he is not so torn between the dualism of his own question and the many answers offered by the multitude of personalities within him. He is interested to discover that he has a rather definite sense of discrimination among all these mystical, Oriental, and esoteric books which he now finds everywhere he goes.

Standing alone in front of a rack of texts dealing with the whole range of the spiritual explosion—from Tibetan Buddhism to astral projection, ancient Sufi texts to books on est or Transcendental Meditation, from the Vedas or the Kabbalah to handbooks on sexual yoga and mind-power; Krishnamurti, Chögyam Trungpa, Muktananda, Vilayat Khan, Idries Shah . . . —he finds in himself very little indecision or difficulty selecting the books he wants to read.

Why is this? How is it that this man who in every other aspect of his life is hurled from one world to another, who can take no stand even in the details of his life, here finds that he knows what he wants?

Of course, very little is as yet actually at stake. It is only a book, only a few dollars. But were he to reflect upon himself he would recognize that something purer is operating in him. An outsider observing him might not be able to distinguish this process from ordinary curiosity or intellectual interest. But inside, the man feels, probably unconsciously, that a certain dream, going far back to his childhood, is now being aroused and nourished. It is the dream of the wise man, the dream of great learning. And it is connected, in a way he does not understand, with the intimate question of his being.

But now a more problematic stage is reached. He begins to be seriously interested in the fact that all around him are followers of spiritual paths. He goes to lectures, begins to ask questions. He meets people who are known as teachers, gurus, or spiritual guides.

Here is a Hindu, just arrived from India. The people around him speak of him as "God-realized," the Master of Masters, the incarnation of the Supreme Reality. Our man is bold enough to ask for a private audience and amid the fumes of incense and the sight of young Americans dressed in robes, amid the chanting of Sanskrit words and the presentations of fruit and flowers, he tries . . . to express . . . his question . . . the question . . . that is himself. He tries to utter the sound of his own being.

Or here is a Buddhist teacher, a man of powerful intellect and quiet yet dramatic energy. He senses that the people surrounding this teacher are saner than he himself is; he feels his own agitation and, through the teacher's presence and attention to him, he grasps that there is a state of consciousness possible in which life could be transformed. He wants to reach for that, but he needs time to think it over; he is afraid of commitment, the commitment he feels he must make deep down in himself. And suddenly does he wonder: what has become of my question? In any case, entering the whirl of his life, it appears again. And he is faced with the possibility of becoming free of his question through the teacher who has so impressed him . . .

Or again, a man who is known as a Sufi teacher . . .

Or now a master without credentials, offering something forged in the present—this teacher, too, has power . . . and knowledge, of this there can be no doubt.

What has become of our man now? This is contemporary America. It is not Tibet or India, or even medieval France. Here he must choose, not only among teachers, but from among traditions, from among whole universes bearing the weight of history and culture not his own; or, if in some sense his own, containing ideas which he can hardly understand, far less accept as true.

Shall he respond to the man or his ideas? Shall he trust his feeling or his thought? He liked that teacher—is that a right basis? He was made uncomfortable by the other—perhaps that is a truer help. This one is a recognized master, authorized, bearing the robe of the lineage—surely one must give that serious weight; the other comes from God knows where, has put together something exciting, but what is it? Can he trust his life to it?

In short, our man has found that worlds-upon-worlds have followed him into the spiritual search. As in his life, he is tossed from one to the other—and this is so even if he chooses to follow this or that leader; in six months, or a year, or five, with whom will he be then? And why? How long to stay, when to give up and try another? Perhaps give up everything and accept life as it is?

But now he has found—because of all this—something exceedingly important, exceedingly subtle and interesting. His question, the question of his being, has not let go of him; it has dogged him into the very pockets of the gods; it is not as fragile as he thought. True, he could not express it, ever, to anyone; but now he knows it is acting upon him; now and then, all too infrequently and lasting perhaps but a moment, it breaks in upon him and gives him the strength to wait, to not choose, to be cautious outwardly because inwardly something very daring is possible: to be silent and alert, ready without tension to move when it is 'ght to move.

The problems of his life now assume a different place. They continue to overwhelm him, to take all his attention, but more and more a thought appears that is energized by what he has seen of himself and suffered of himself. His question is now seeking to break through more and more—perhaps it happens in his dreams, what were once called sacred dreams, the dreams that awaken a man from sleep rather than protect his sleep as do the dreams of fallen-away man.

And it is here that we who are pondering the question of the search for the wise man must stop and reflect perhaps upon the harmony of psyche and cosmos of which our Hermetic diagrams are speaking. What force, beyond psychology, is moving in this man, who, let us hope, is also ourselves? Where does it come from and toward what great unity, unknown under the names of happiness and satisfaction, is it driving? And if this is a universe of conscious law, drawing all beings upward who seek to be drawn, and even those, in the end, who do not seek, but only wish to seek—if this is such a universe, and if our earth is part of that universe, how can we not imagine that all around are helping powers waiting for us to raise our hand blindly up, the hand of our being, my own question which comes not from the psyche, but from the subtle and fleeting and mercifully-given-by-life destruction of my psyche?

It is said, "When the pupil is ready, the teacher appears." How could we now think of this as anything but a cosmic law, which means that no outer conditions arranged by human history can stand in its way? Yet obviously, man—I, myself—can stand in its way. How?

In this way. For let us conclude by considering that all the wise men or teachers now in our midst are authentic—forgetting for a moment that there are such things as frauds, charlatans, imposters. Forget also the notion of a teaching or teacher suited to my particular needs, or the needs of this era. Consider only that the intelligence and spiritual instinct I need is given by my question, it is not something I can develop or improve upon by my own efforts. Now, here, pondering what to do, how to seek, whom to choose, I make my move. I see that in that movement, that impulse of reaching out, I have lost my question, I am no longer in the center of the question of my being.

But seeing that, accepting that I am again lost in the illusions of decision, my question instantly returns. Then, and only then, can I ask for a guide; and then, and only then, so it is said, reality is obliged to yield the guide up to me.

REFERENCES

Illustration: Twelfth-century Hermetic manuscript (MS Lat. 3236A) Bibliothèque Nationale, Paris. Photograph: Bibliothèque Nationale, Paris.

1. Sri Krishna Prem, *The Yoga of the Bhagavad Gita* (Baltimore: Penguin Books, 1973).
2. Heinrich Zimmer, *Philosophies of India,* ed. Joseph Campbell (Princeton: Princeton University Press, 1969), pp. 51–52.
3. *The Life of Milarepa,* trans. Lobsang P. Lhalungpa (London: Granada Publishing, 1979), p. xv.
4. Zimmer, *Philosophies of India,* p. 56.
5. Henry Corbin, *The Man of Light in Iranian Sufism* (Boulder, Colo: Shambhala, 1978).

GURDJIEFF, OUSPENSKY, AND ESOTERIC PHILOSOPHY

I SHOULD like to begin by examining the phrase, "esoteric philosophy," which has lately been delivered like a foundling onto our doorstep. I am inclined to take the child in. But first, and before speaking about the ideas of Gurdjieff, I am going to make an honest effort to locate the infant's proper parents to see if perhaps they haven't had a change of heart and really want their child back. If not, I suppose we shall have to adopt this conceptual orphan as our own.

It is clearly a case of mixed parentage. The term "philosophy," although it originally meant the striving for wisdom, has in modern times come to mean principally conceptual analysis and speculative explanation. Philosophy as the search for ideas that can guide the conduct of human life has long since been relegated to the status of an anachronism. To the modern mind, such a task is the province of parental training, religion or, in adults, psychotherapy. The task of philosophy is now to explore presuppositions or argue on the truth or falsity of concepts about man, morality, God, and nature. It is simply assumed that man lives according to his ideas; the point is to attain correct and adequate ideas, and the conduct of life will take care of itself—although perhaps with a little help from our friends, religion and psychotherapy. The penetration of ideas into the heart and body of man is not generally considered at issue; it is never really discussed.

As for the "esoteric," we need not trouble ourselves at the outset with considering the popular connotations of this term, as when it is used to refer to highly technical knowledge and language which only a handful of trained specialists understand. Taken in this way, the term more often than not has a pejorative cast to it, and is often associated with the even more dubious term "occultism." No, let us rather get right to the issue and come back later if we really want to, to an examination of the negative, the justifiably negative, associations which we bring to such terms as "esotericism," "secret knowledge," "hidden wisdom," etc., in modern times.

The point is that, in its real root meaning, the term "esoteric" refers directly to this question of living according to great and true ideas. "The good that I would I do not: but the evil which I would not, that I do." "For I delight in the law of God after the inward man. But I see another law in my members, warring against the law of my mind, and bringing me into captivity to the law of sin . . ." The "inward man" of St. Paul translates the Greek *ho eso anthropos,* that deeply interior and generally hidden aspect of the human structure which knows and senses what is true and good, but which, in our degraded state, is powerless and even unknown in our actual lives as we live them. The term "esoteric" is inseparable from recognition of *ho eso anthropos.* To speak of an inner knowledge is to speak also of an inner man. To speak of a hidden knowledge is also to speak of a hidden part of ourselves which is more truly ourselves than the personal identity which we acquire in society. Esoteric knowledge and practices refer, therefore, to the struggle that is necessary in order for man to penetrate beneath the carapace of the surface personality to *ho eso anthropos,* and so that a relationship can be built between the inner and the outer elements of the human structure.

What then could be the meaning of the term "esoteric philosophy"? Philosophy in its accepted modern forms simply does not recognize *ho eso anthropos.* Yes, one does find from Hume to Kant and throughout twentieth-century philosophy much discussion of what is called "the problem of the self." And, yes, existentialists and phenomenologists have spoken of the authentic self and the transcendental ego. But *ho eso anthropos* is none of these; in fact, to theorize and speculate and argue about it may simply be to cover it over with yet another veil. The error here, and it is an error not simply of thought, but an error of life, is to identify the realm of thought, emotion, and sensation as the inner world of man. *Ho eso anthropos* is not a thought, nor even the power of thought itself; not emotion and not perception and not sensation—nor all of these in the aggregate.

To say that philosophy as we know it does not recognize the inner man is to imply ultimately that the fundamental questions of life, the questions human beings can ask with the whole of themselves, cannot be answered or even approached through a part of the mind that analyzes, compares, and explains. The term "esoteric" invites us, therefore, to consider those moments of life in which *ho eso anthropos* appears in our own experience and consciousness as an active force.

In saying this, worlds upon worlds of human experience suddenly open up before us as material for pondering the question of the inner and outer conditions under which in fact we human beings do approach the ability to live according to truth and value. Philosophy, considered as an attempt to analyze and organize ordinary experience, falls away. Such philosophy is an outward-directed influence in human life and directs our attention in a completely opposite direction from the esoteric. It assumes we have an inner self always accessible and active in our lives; or at least that it is a matter of our willing and choosing to obey it. It gives the name "reason" to this innermost part of us and identifies this reason as our highest part. It assumes that we live according to truth when we can explain and clarify the truth, and when we will it. In such philosophy there is no room for the upheaval of a St. Paul confronting the total helplessness of man in body, will, and thought to manifest in accordance with truth.

The parents of our foundling term "esoteric philosophy" have now been identified. The esoteric seeks to remind us of and even evoke in us a simultaneous sense of the real world calling to us from within and the illusory world in which we live and move throughout our lives. This it does by communications addressed to a part of the self that is almost always hidden from our awareness or which, even when it appears in the course of life, is not honored or valued or correctly named. Philosophy, on the other hand, in its accepted forms, draws our attention into the intellectual process which is as powerless in the inner world of man as it is powerful in the outer world of nature. Thought, by itself, cannot transform human nature. When Eastern teachings speak of the thinking process as on the same level as the five senses, these teachings are stating, among other things, just this very point about the structural limitations of our ordinary intellectual activity, no matter how brilliant and impassioned it may be.

To complete our identification of the parentage of the term "esoteric philosophy," it is necessary now to draw an important distinction that will also help orient us toward the Gurdjieff teaching. We may say that the esoteric refers to energy while philosophy refers to concepts, formulations, words. And we may distinguish philosophy from the esoteric by saying that the latter is the study leading to the transformation of intrapsychic energies, whereas the former, philosophy, is the clarification and development of concepts. Putting the issue in this way helps us to understand why the esoteric traditions, if we may use that word, are always associated with what is called oral transmission—why the written word plays only a part in the awakening of *ho eso anthropos*. Oral transmission, let us be clear, refers to personal, direct contact with a guide and community and to the entire set of conditions of living and human interaction established in the community. Only in conditions that touch the whole of human life can the energies within the human self be brought to light and integrated, that is, transformed.

What is the relationship between energy and thought? That is the question brought home to us by the term we are considering, "esoteric philosophy." I may think well and truly, but at the same time I may forever lack the mastery or centralization of human energy that will enable me to act and be in accordance with what I know mentally. The good that I would do, that I do not. If this is the human condition, then it will change me not at all to have only new and better concepts to think about, or even new and higher objects of emotion. It is a question of establishing a vital center of action within the self, not of finding new objects upon which to direct my present weak and dissipating energies of thinking and feeling. Therefore, if the term "esoteric philosophy" is to have real meaning, it will surely be as part of the study of the relationship between concepts and human energy, the study, to use a Gurdjieff term, of what brings moral power into the life of the human individual.

Energy and thought are the parents of esoteric philosophy. As a man, I seek this study and I hope for the harmonization within myself of these two fundamental aspects of my own being; but as an academician, I find myself backing away from it. The university is not a school of awakening; professors are not spiritual guides and, as I am sure we can all agree, the books we write are not scripture.

An anecdote of Hasidic origin will help to illustrate my point. The *rebbe* is asked the following question by a pupil, referring to Deuteronomy 6:6: *And these words, which I command thee this day, shall be upon thy heart.* "Why is it said this way?" the pupil asks. "Why are we told to put these words *upon* our heart? Why are we not told to place them *in* our heart?" To this, the *rebbe* answers that it is not within man's power to place the divine teachings directly in his heart. "All that we can do is place them on the surface of the heart so that when the heart breaks they will drop in."

Of all those figures whom we call philosophers throughout our history it was surely Socrates who understood this fact about the relationship between thought and energy. Before great ideas can enter into the bones and blood of man the heart must break. That is to say, man must confront his own ignorance and illusions about everything existing in the world, but principally about himself. In the state of ontological self-questioning, a power of mind appears, a new and central attention which simultaneously exposes the fragmentation of the ego while pointing the way to the existence within myself of *ho eso anthropos*. The development and strengthening of this central attention in order to forge a bridge between man's two natures may be understood as the primary aim of those disciplines which can rightfully be called esoteric.

This is no simple task. The demand it places upon the searcher is extraordinary, and, as Plato informs us, it is for the few, not for the many. In the whole corpus of the Platonic writings there are only two places where he demonstrates something of what is required of the true lover of wisdom, the true philosopher. One of these descriptions occurs in the *Phaedo* and *Crito* where the reader sees himself in the struggle of the pupils of Socrates who both do and do not accept the mode in which the teacher accepts death. The bittersweet poignancy of this characterization of the death of Socrates is known to all of us, so much so that in certain respects its effect is comparable to the immeasurable shock delivered to the mind and heart of man by the passion of Christ in which any serious man can glimpse in himself the immensity of the struggle between the two natures and their possible reconciliation.

The other description of this process of ontological self-questioning is also well known, but is often misunderstood. It occurs at the end of the *Symposium* where the figure of Alcibiades is introduced as a paradigm of man standing between his own two natures and turning away in shame from the lifelong struggle that it lays open to him. Alcibiades is often merely interpreted as a man of great brilliance giving himself to a life of dissolution. It is true—he is dissolute; but what is even more important is that he sees this in himself with crushing clarity, and this constatation of his own level of being lifts his refusal of Socrates above the pallid acceptance of Socrates by other figures in the Platonic dialogues, and also unites him to Socrates himself who understands that the awareness of one's own nothingness and self-illusion is precisely the foundation of the search for wisdom (defined as the complete internalization of true ideas).

It is in this context that I am able to see the relevance of Gurdjieff to the study of philosophical ideas. Gurdjieff's early life, as recounted in his partly allegorical autobiographical work *Meetings with Remarkable Men*, offers the portrait of a search for knowledge conducted with such all-round intensity that this search itself becomes an ontologically transforming force. In this book, a specific quality of searching is revealed as the real beginning in the life of man of what we are terming *ho eso anthropos*. Whether it was the teachings of science or the doctrines of religion, or occult phenomena such as table tapping, precognition, and apparent cases of survival after death, the young Gurdjieff is portrayed always as seeking, questioning, drawn by a vision of knowledge which will not be satisfied by anything short of concrete certainty about the whole meaning of man's life on earth. The modern reader, puzzled by the fragmentation of contemporary scientific knowledge, disillusioned by the powerlessness of modern religious doctrines, intrigued but skeptical about the claims of mysticism and occultism, emerges from this book with a unique sense of self-permission not communicated, in my experience, by any other document of our times. The reader is *permitted* once again to ask questions of a kind and in a manner that he has long since ceased to ask. I mean to say, he is permitted to ask fundamental questions in the way he asked them, perhaps, only as a child, in those moments when the sense of "I, myself" appeared under the rubric of uncomplicated wonder and sorrow. I think you know what I am speaking about here.

This is not idealism in its conventional meaning. Nevertheless, the permission to ask great questions with the whole of one's presence implies, but does not insist upon, the existence of great answers. It implies it only, because in no other way can it be communicated that the great answers require not only profound formulations of ideas, but also and equally, the development in oneself of what Gurdjieff called the *being* of a man, the growth of *I am,* the real self.

I have said that philosophy as we know it does not recognize *ho eso anthropos.* But now I wish to go further with this thought. *Ho eso anthropos,* the inner man, is not yet *I am.* It is the seed, the impulse of the fully developed inner reality of human nature. As a seed, as a weak impulse, faintly heard, it is powerless. It needs to grow, develop into the maturity of inner *dynamis* or energy signified in Christian doctrines, as it seems to me, by the distinction between man as image of God and man as likeness of God. Therefore, while it is a tremendous omission not to recognize nor speak to this incipient inner impulse called *ho eso anthropos*—and this is the distinct limitation of philosophy in its known and accepted forms— it is an error of equal consequence to speak to man as though this *ho eso anthropos* were already fully developed and situated in the place of power and efficacy within our structure.

The task of the esoteric is therefore quite specific and extraordinarily subtle: to speak to the inner man as a present weak fact and a possible future power. Thus the esoteric is *not* the mystical. Mystical religion and philosophy speak to man as though he were already in the likeness of God; as though he were already *I am* in the sense that the highest principle in the universe is *I am,* as God identifies his nature to Moses: "Thou shalt say unto the children of Israel, I AM hath sent me unto you" (Exodus 3:14).

To awaken and support the act of self-interrogation as a force that is itself the seed of the *I am:* I take this to be the aim of the esoteric as it finds its way into the general turnover of human life. But actually to guide this work of self-interrogation in its practical details so that it becomes a new way of life and an avenue to the eventual transformation of man's being: this I take to be the function, in part, of what Gurdjieff's most famous pupil, P. D. Ouspensky, called a *school.*

To ask about esoteric philosophy is therefore to ask what sort of ideas, in what sort of formulation, can help to awaken ontological self-questioning—the stirring of *ho eso anthropos.* I believe it was this sort of issue that drove Kierkegaard to attack the Hegelian philosophy and all it represented as, if we may so express it, an enormous system of answers that actually crushed the question, which is the seed of authentic individual being. Surely, Kierkegaard's method of indirect communication must, at least partially, be understood in this light, as must the Platonic portrayal of Socratic method which he drew on, as well as Plato's usage, at carefully determined places in the dialogues, of myth and dramatic exchange.

If I now attempt to sum up the ideas of Gurdjieff about the universe and man's possible development, it is only to emphasize the extent to which he presented these ideas in a manner and under conditions inextricably linked to the aim of awakening the search for the *I am.* Today, people from varied backgrounds are beginning to detect something in the Gurdjieff teaching that is intimately recognizable as their own although they have great difficulty justifying it by conventional standards of scholarship or argument. Christians may sense in his ideas what he himself referred to as "esoteric Christianity"; Buddhists detect something similar with respect to his teachings about the nature of the false self and his methods of self-observation; others see Sufi origins; still others see the real and long-lost origins of the scientific attitude toward life and nature as taught by Pythagoras and Socrates. But when the Gurdjieff teaching was first becoming known half a century ago, the situation was apparently quite different—no one could recognize it as anything known at all: it was neither religion nor science nor philosophy. In fact, both responses taken together no doubt represent the specific response to the esoteric in its immediate, living form. We may imagine that those who chose to follow Gurdjieff both did and did not recognize the nature of his ideas and person. This is to say that every great system of ideas about man and the universe and every formulation of an overall attitude toward life—be it religious, philosophical, or scientific—eventually become absorbed into the functions of the outer man, the agents of the soul, in Meister Eckhardt's meaning of the term. All truth becomes acceptable in the sense that its formulations are absorbed by the functions of thinking or emotion. Behind these functions, however, lies *ho eso anthropos,* the seed of *I am.* The individual who is moved by this incipient impulse toward the real heart of the human structure simultaneously feels that he both is and is not himself; he is torn between two natures, two movements within the composition of every human being. And any teaching that truly deserves the name esoteric must surely be that which evokes this inbetweenness corresponding to the actual human condition as we are.

To date, there has been only one summation of the teaching of Gurdjieff that also conveys something of this double-natured communication, namely, P. D. Ouspensky's *In Search of the Miraculous.*

The book is written in the form of a personal account of Ouspensky's years with Gurdjieff, and the ideas of Gurdjieff are presented to some extent in their chronological sequence against the background of the conditions of life which Gurdjieff created for his pupils during the chaos and upheaval of prerevolutionary Russia. In addition to being a faithful presentation of the Gurdjieff system, the book thereby also provides much material about the life of Gurdjieff and the early history of what has now become known as "the work."

The book's form also allows Ouspensky to communicate to the reader what he clearly considers to be the necessary emotional correlates of these ideas. This is done with refreshing honesty and extraordinary skill—and in a variety of ways—often through Ouspensky's describing the difficulties he and others encountered in understanding an idea, or the shock when understanding finally appeared and, often, the sense of joy or urgency when realizing this was the great knowledge, the miraculous, of which one had dreamed, but that the demands it made upon the seeker were correspondingly awesome.

Great care is taken throughout the book to characterize the master-pupil relationship between Gurdjieff and his circle. The resulting picture of Gurdjieff is of a man obviously possessing immense wisdom and personal power, capable at once of painfully stripping away the pupil's "mask" while carefully guiding him through the emotional and bodily experiences necessary for the process of deep learning. The information and speculations which Ouspensky offers about the sources of Gurdjieff's knowledge and about his motivations for acting as he did in various situations, rather than satisfying the reader's curiosity about Gurdjieff, communicate instead the impression of an indecipherable man, doubtless one of the most enigmatic men of the twentieth century.

Finally, the form of the book allows Ouspensky to present the Gurd-jieff ideas in a specific psychological sequence and in carefully selected juxtapositions without calling this strategy to the attention of the reader.

As for the contents of the book, it touches on nothing less than the whole of the vast Gurdjieffian philosophy, cosmology, psychology, and guidelines for living. Although the book's subtitle, "Fragments of an Un-known Teaching," is presumably meant to indicate that the connected-ness between all the various ideas cannot be made intellectually explicit, but must be discovered through experience, and although from a certain point of view it must still be considered a preliminary treatment, never-theless the impression of an awesomely comprehensive system of ideas is inescapable. What follows is necessarily an extremely truncated ab-stract:

The author begins by describing his first meeting with Gurdjieff shortly after he, Ouspensky, had returned from India in search of a school of higher knowledge. To Ouspensky's surprise, this man Gurd-jieff, whom he is meeting in his native Russia, seems to possess that knowledge which Ouspensky had twice traveled around the world seek-ing. Moreover, Gurdjieff has organized a group, structured along un-familiar but intriguing principles, to study this knowledge. There are es-oteric schools, Gurdjieff tells him, but the first thing to realize is that a very special sort of knowledge is needed, even among esoteric teachings, in order for a man to have results corresponding to his full possibilities. And the first thing necessary is for a man to see how far in fact he is from these possibilities. Man, says Gurdjieff, is actually not a man, he is a machine. All the attributes of man—freedom, understanding, love, cre-ativity—are not his until he works for them. Man can cease to be a ma-chine; he can become conscious. But first he must see his complete me-chanicalness. This is extremely difficult, and very few can wish for or bear to see the truth about themselves.

Conversations with Gurdjieff continue until gradually a group forms itself for the sake of studying and putting the ideas into practice. Man's possibilities are very great, Gurdjieff tells them, greater than they can imagine. It is, he says, a question of actually forming within oneself something tangibly permanent, something higher and more real than the physical body which is all there is of ordinary man, no matter what he may imagine of himself. Gurdjieff presents to Ouspensky's group the teaching about the soul that can be developed in man, and this is juxta-posed to Gurdjieff's teaching about the aim of his work—namely, the development of *being* in man. Man *is* not; he is only a fragmented and veiled collection of personages masquerading as a real self. The real self must be formed through work, through a specific form of suffering, a discipline. Such discipline lies at the heart of the great traditions, but this path does not exist in the modern, Western world. At the same time, there can be several forms of this discipline, some quick and some slow, some suitable for modern man, some unsuitable. Gurdjieff describes his teaching as representing the *fourth way,* not the way of bodily struggle (the way of the fakir), nor the way of emotional devotion (the way of the monk), nor the way of the development of reason (the way of the yogi). The fourth way works on all aspects of man at the same time, and requires no renunciation or belief. It can be and indeed must be practiced in the midst of ordinary life conditions. It is thus easier and faster, but also, in another sense, far more difficult than the traditionally recognized methods of self-development. The difficulty consists in its inherent newness—it can never be a culturally familiar form, but must always move at a different tempo from human culture or the normally recognized functions of reason; because it is the rapid path, it puts constant pressure upon the individual for seeing the truth about himself.

Gurdjieff also speaks about the absence of unity in another, more fundamental way which also points to the meaning, in this teaching, of man's potentially developed unity. The human structure, Ouspensky and his group learn, consists of several minds. These minds, or *centers* of perception, are the real structural elements of human nature and any attempts to bring man to unity that do not understand these centers are bound to fail.

At various points throughout the book, the subject of the centers (basically, the thinking center, the emotional center, and the moving-instinctive center), is treated and developed more and more until it becomes clear that the idea of the three centers in man is one of the most central ideas in the whole of the Gurdjieffian system. Man's confusion, his lack of unity, his unnecessary suffering, his immorality—in fact everything that characterizes the sorrow of the human condition—come about because these centers of perception are wrongly related, wrongly functioning, and because man does not see or care to know this about himself.

A characteristic of *In Search of the Miraculous,* which from all other accounts doubtless reflects the Gurdjieff teaching accurately, is the unique mingling of cosmological ideas with teachings concerning psychology. Ouspensky now begins the long, powerful portrayal of Gurdjieff's teachings about the origin and structure of the universe, the laws behind the appearances, laws and forces that govern everything from the creation of galaxies to the movements of atoms to the energy transactions within the human organism.

The two basic laws of reality are *the law of three forces* and *the law of the octave*. Every phenomenon in the universe is inevitably the manifestation of three forces; and every process takes place according to a structure symbolized by the familiar seven-tone musical scale, with steps either upward or downward and with junctures, or *intervals*, where the development of forces is checked and requires special new energy to proceed along its original path.

Ouspensky painstakingly states these ideas while taking every opportunity to quote Gurdjieff's dictum that the only way an individual can understand these cosmic laws is to observe them in himself, and this through the special forms of the "work" which are rapidly developing in the group of which Ouspensky is a member. Meanwhile, the reader is made aware that revolution and war are moving close; all around the madness of mankind is becoming more and more apparent.

Like the idea of the centers, once the ideas of the law of three forces and the law of the octave are introduced they become a permanent part of all future discussion. On their basis is built the whole of Gurdjieff's teachings about the levels and movement between levels in the universe, from the absolute through the systems of the stars, suns, and planets down to the earth and, finally, the moon. The ray of creation or chain of worlds is ruled by the same laws that govern the inner and outer life of man and everything in surrounding nature.

For all the vastness and complexity of the material based upon these laws, however, it soon becomes clear that the most essential issue to be understood is the relationship of these laws to the nearly insoluble difficulty in which man finds himself—his prison of lies, fears, and self-deception, his state of *sleep,* and the need for him to begin the long and difficult work of awakening to himself and of developing in himself the powers and functions which are proper to man, the "crown of creation."

There now proceeds a discussion of the structure of the human organism seen in the light of the universal laws of the transformation of energy. The food man eats, the air he breathes, and the impressions he experiences are intimately interconnected as forms by which energies are accepted into the organism and assimilated or rejected. This is the idea of the "three foods" of man, and much of the Gurdjieff teaching is understandable only on the basis of this idea—for example, the reason he places complete emphasis on consciousness as seeing, rather than on efforts of man to make changes in himself. The deepest and most important change of human nature comes about, according to Gurdjieff, through the assimilation of the energy of impressions, and this takes place through the work of awareness without dire efforts to make changes. This work of awareness, called here *self-remembering,* is the principal instrument by means of which man may accumulate the force necessary for the eventual manifestation in himself of the properties of will, creative intelligence, conscience, and the power to love one's fellow man.

A rather extensive description of the workings of a Gurdjieff group is now given and is connected to many essential and new ideas—for example, the idea that an esoteric school also is structured along the lines of cosmic law in all its aspects. The most crucial idea here, which has already been introduced but is now given a telling practical import, is Gurdjieff's teaching about evolution. He uses this term in a way strikingly different from that of modern science and different also from its current use among followers of the new religions. According to Gurdjieff, there are two major forces in the universe—the force by which the absolute manifests, which is a movement from higher to lower, from simplicity to complexity; and a movement back toward the source, a movement upward, toward the unity of simplicity. The latter is evolution, the former involution.

Past a certain stage, evolution is not and cannot be automatic, mechanical; it requires special work and conscious discipline. It can only proceed through individual human beings working together. In short, the evolution of man is neither the mechanical, biological process of modern science, nor the social or planetary phenomenon of the contemporary Aquarians. The fascinating details of the structure of Gurdjieff groups that appear in this portion of Ouspensky's book are more understandable when it is seen that human evolution requires extraordinary conditions of individual and collective effort, conditions which go against the grain of every known psychological, religious, or social organization.

In the latter half of the book numerous ideas are introduced which both amplify those already given and at the same time provide a completely new angle of vision on the whole system and which also seem an integral part of the whole. There is something about the intensity and underlying urgency with which this book is written that gives each portion the rather rare characteristic of seeming new on each reading, just as the whole system keeps being redefined over the course of Ouspensky's years with Gurdjieff.

We are introduced to the idea of essence and personality, the division of human nature between what is man's own and what he acquires; we learn of the existence and role of other centers besides the three basic centers. One of the most dramatic and personal sections of the book occurs in this latter part—where Ouspensky vividly describes experiences of an inexplicable nature regarding his relationship with Gurdjieff, experiences or facts which Gurdjieff had promised him would eventually come. It is clear that Ouspensky in this case seeks to portray a personal state of consciousness which he believes is unlike anything in the known mystical literature of the world. More than anything else, however, personal relations described in this latter part of the book partake of a unique quality of feeling which may strike the reader as puzzling, even chilling, yet perhaps also as evidencing new possibilities of the reach of the human heart. Ouspensky's decision to leave his teacher, poignantly but tersely described toward the very end of the book, has this same ambiguity in the most extreme degree. Has Gurdjieff veered away from a certain right direction? Or has he brought Ouspensky to a stage of inner development which can only proceed further through the creation in the pupil of an entirely new and unknown human emotion?

Chief among the new ideas introduced in this portion of the book is the mysterious nine-pointed diagram known as the *enneagram*. As explained by Ouspensky in several sections, it is an ancient symbol, never before made known, which represents the fundamental laws of transformation that have already been described in the whole of the book. It is thus *par excellence* Gurdjieff's diagram of the organic unity of everything existing: the law of three forces, the law of seven, the processes of assimilating the three "foods," the patterns governing the transmission of esoteric knowledge, and the structural dynamics of every living thing in nature, including the incomplete being, man, myself.

INDEX